LISTEN

TO

THE ECHO

LISTEN
TO
THE ECHO

Truth & Justice Betrayed

DENNIS JAMES HAUT

authorHOUSE®

AuthorHouse™
1663 Liberty Drive
Bloomington, IN 47403
www.authorhouse.com
Phone: 1-800-839-8640

First published by AuthorHouse   08/22//2011

ISBN: 978-1-4634-4544-7 (sc)
ISBN: 978-1-4634-4545-4 (ebk)

Library of Congress Control Number: 2011914118

Printed in the United States of America

CONTENTS

DEDICATION

ECHO IS DEDICATED TO THE ONE PERSON WHO DESERVES MY RECOGNITION. THAT PERSON IS MY ONE TRUE LOVE, GLORIA JOAN HAUT, FOR HER BELIEVING AND STANDING WITH ME NO MATTER WHAT THE COST. WE LOST HUNDREDS OF THOUSANDS OVER THE LAST SEVEN YEARS BECAUSE OF AN INCOMPETENT ATTORNEY, A STATE COURT SYSTEM THAT'S NOT WORTH HAVING AND LAW ENFORCEMENT OFFICERS JUST NOT DOING THEIR JOB, A BIAS JUDGE IGNORING THE LAW AND THE MICHIGAN SUPREME COURT DECISION, AND JUDAH.

MANY YEARS AGO, AS A GOVERNMENT TEACHER, I TAUGHT WHAT WAS SUPPOSE TO BE. NOW, THE PICTURE HAS DRASTICALLY CHANGED. AMERICAN GOVERNMENT SHOULD NOT AND WOULD NOT BE TAUGHT THE SAME TODAY AS IT WAS IN THE PAST. PEOPLE DON'T SEEM TO CARE ABOUT

EACH OTHER ANYMORE. OUR SOCIETY HAS CHANGED FOR THE WORSE.

WHAT MY GENERATION WAS TAUGHT IS NOT BEING PASSED ONTO OUR FUTURE LEADERS. MOTHERS AND FATHERS OF TODAY ARE TO BUSY TRYING TO KEEP UP INSTEAD OF MAKING SURE THE GOOD THINGS ARE BEING PASSED FROM GENERATION TO GENERATION.

I BELIEVE OUR ONCE GREAT DEMOCRACY IS A THING OF THE PAST. IT WILL NEVER AGAIN BE THE WAY OUR FOREFATHERS INTENDED IT TO BE. I HAVE ALWAYS TRIED TO DO WHAT WAS RIGHT NO MATTER WHAT THE PRICE AND ECHO WILL DEMONSTRATE EXAMPLE AFTER EXAMPLE OF EXACTLY WHAT I MEAN. I HAVE ALWAYS BELIEVED THAT TRUTH AND HONESTY WILL ALWAYS PREVAIL OVER EVIL AND INJUSTICE WITHIN OUR GREAT SOCIETY. MY AMERICAN DREAM HAS CHANGED FOR THE WORSE. I HAVE FINALLY COME TO THE CONCLUSION THAT THE AMERICAN DREAM IS NOT FOR AMERICANS. THE GOVERNMENT WANTS YOU TO BELIEVE THIS BUT ACTIONS SPEAK LOUDER THAN WORDS. I BELIEVE THE

AMERICAN PUBLIC FOR THE MOST PART HAS NOW CAUGHT ON. THINGS ARE ABOUT TO HAPPEN.

CORRUPTION AND GREED ARE NOW THE RULE OF THUMB. IT'S SO DEEP IN OUR SOCIETY IT WILL NEVER TRULY CHANGE UNTIL WE HIT ROCK BOTTOM. OUR GOVERNMENT ONLY TELLS US WHAT THEY WANT US TO KNOW AND NOT WHAT'S REALLY TAKING PLACE ON THE LOCAL, STATE AND NATIONAL LEVEL. ECHO IS ABOUT THE THINGS I HAVE WITNESSED AND LIVED WITH MY ENTIRE LIFE. IT DEPICTS WHAT I KNOW ABOUT TWO DIFFERENT EDUCATIONAL SYSTEMS IN THE STATE OF MICHIGAN THAT ARE NOT AS FAR APART AS MOST PEOPLE THINK. THEY ARE ACTUALLY THE SAME IN MOST RESPECTS AS DEMONSTRATED WITHIN THE FOLLOWING PAGES. I SPENT THIRTY-FOUR YEARS IN THE EDUCATIONAL FIELD. THIRTY-TWO YEARS AS A HIGH SCHOOL PRINCIPAL THAT I REALLY ENJOYED. MY CAREER CAME TO AN ABRUPT END FOR NO REASON THAT THIS BOOK WILL EXPLAIN IN GREATER DETAIL. IT HAS TAKEN ME NEARLY SEVEN YEARS

TO THINK ABOUT WHAT ACTUALLY TOOK PLACE AND THE EVENTS THAT LED TO MY RETIREMENT IN 2004. I WOULD MOST LIKELY STILL BE WORKING IN EDUCATION IF THE DECISION WERE MINE ALONE. THIS BOOK WILL NOW TELL YOU THE TRUTH OF WHAT ACTUALLY TOOK PLACE WITHIN THE TWO EDUCATIONAL INSTITUTIONS I WORKED IN UNTIL THE DAY I HAD TO RETIRE TO KEEP MY HEAD ABOVE WATER. NAMES HAVE BEEN CHANGED TO PROTECT THE INNOCENT CHILDREN OF GOD.

Chapter I

THINGS REMEMBERED BUT NEVER FORGOTTEN

COPY MACHINE

I walked into my office on a Monday morning and everything seemed normal until I started the new Xerox machine. I noticed the machine was tampered with and the lid was broken. I called Father Robert DeLong the associate pastor of St. Stephen Church to see if he knew anything about what had happened. He told me that he had no idea and knew nothing.

I decided that the best thing to do at this point was to contact the local police to investigate the situation. Before doing this, I noticed something under the broken lid. It was a student's transcript from St. Peter and Paul's Seminary. This was another high school in the Saginaw Area that Father Bob was the chaplain for. I knew he was connected with what had happened but he was not about to admit it and I decided to make a call to St. Petes and talk with Sr. Reda the principal. I decided to just have the copy machine fixed when I figured out what was going on.

Sister Reda was in my office before I could turn around. She had already knew who was the guilty party because he had been giving her a hard time about everything. I gave her the boy's transcript and explained what was going on.

Sr. Reda had been a principal for quite some time and knew what she was doing. She told me Father Bob was writing this boy a recommendation for college because she refused to. Father Bob was the type of priest who thought his involvement with the students should never be questioned. He was the pastor of St. Petes and he could do whatever he wanted. He thought he had the blessing of Jesus himself and he acted as such. Sr. Reda called me later and told me she was going to the Bishop. Her intention was to have Bishop Ken Ulander get rid of Father Bob as the chaplain of her school. I tried to tell her that the Bishop never went against his priests. He didn't have enough of them to service his public. She pushed ahead anyways. In the spring of that same year I heard that she had been dismissed and would no longer be Principal of Sts. Peter and Paul High School. We lost a good one over a situation caused by Father Bob.

CHAPTER II

BETRAYED

SKI TRIP

Later that same year it was now my turn. Father Bob was the type of priest that never backed off and pushed himself way beyond things he knew. He loved to snow ski and decided to take some students on a trip up north to really ski and get to be a good friend with students he did not know that well. He came to my office to let me know his plan. I told him I was not into skiing and I was against what he was trying to do. Students didn't need him as a friend and his control of them was non-existent. He took the issue to the school board as you might expect. I told the Board why I was against the idea and didn't want the school to get involved. The Board decided to sponsor the weekend trip and go against my wishes.

I believe around 80 students signed up for the trip and Father Bob was in his glory. I decided to have a meeting with all the students who had signed up before they left for the weekend trip to Gaylord, Michigan. My purpose was to let the students know that this trip was being sponsored by the school because the Board decided to get involved.

The Board thought with Father Bob in charge the students would not cause any trouble. I explained to the students that the rules of the school would be followed. The punishments for smoking and/or drinking would carry a first time three-day suspension from school. The students and their parents all agreed by signing an agreement that the student handbook would be followed. I later talked with Father Bob and told him to check the student's luggage. Any student being caught with alcohol or tobacco of any type would not be allowed to go on the bus and their parents would be called to take them home before departing. Father Bob agreed and he told me he and the two teachers going along would check all the students out. I told him that the boys would be easier to catch but the girls were a little smarter. The girls would put their liquor in mouthwash bottles along with other plastic or bottles put inside whatever luggage they were carrying. Athletic bags can carry a lot of things besides equipment. Father Bob and I also agreed if anyone were caught their parents would be called to pick them up and take them home. I thought I had covered all my bases and had to allow the trip to go on because of the Board's vote.

Father Bob chose not to search the student's luggage as the students loaded the bus. The only logical conclusion I could draw from his actions was what I feared the most. He wanted to be their friend instead of the authority figure we had agreed upon. This action would prove to be a fatal mistake on his part. Word must have gotten to the students before they left for the trip. Father Bob called me at home as they arrived in Gaylord. He said he could smell liquor on the students as they passed him at the hotel. He decided to have a meeting with the students and asked them to turn in any booze they had and put it on his bed. He told the students no questions would be asked and that would be the end of the issue. As it turned out, twenty-seven bottles of liquor were put on his bed. All but one was never opened. Word went out among the students one bottle was opened and pissed in by one of the students. The student thought if anyone drank his bottle they would drink his piss along with the liquor.

On Friday night Father Bob called me at home. I told Father Bob to bring the students home and we would deal with the situation on Monday morning. The amount of liquor was so much something had to be done. Remember the type of person Bob was. He would not take orders or listen to anyone he thought was less than he was. He chose to keep the trip as it was planned and have the students go skiing instead of listening to me. The thing he did not know was the students only turned in about half the liquor and no beer. The students had a great party for the rest of the weekend and Father Bob had no idea of what they were doing. I was just thankful that nobody was hurt or got into any serious trouble with the law.

Monday morning came and I arrived in school early so I could go to the rectory and talk with Father Bob before I met with the students who went on the trip. Father Bob had the 27 bottles of liquor that were turned in and we sat down to talk. The first thing he said was he wanted the students burned for what they had done. His reputation was on the line and the students stabbed him in the back. He wanted the students punished at any cost and wanted their parents to participate in the punishment. I believe he knew some parents gave the booze to their children for the trip. Some others had fake ID to purchase more booze up north. I agreed with what Father Bob wanted. I told him I would have to think everything over and I would

5

keep him informed before taking any action. I could see we had to stick together on any decisions we made. He agreed and I went back to my office at the school.

I knew the students would be coming to school any time now. I am not the type of administrator that jumps into a hot situation without gathering all the information I can. I decided to talk with the student council president first and see what he knew. I knew I had a great relationship with the president and trusted his opinion. I now had the 27 bottles of liquor in my office and he knew about the one bottle that was opened. We agreed to open and pour out every bottle in the bathroom next to my office. The drains were not going to freeze that winter.

My major problem now was trying to determine who was guilty and who was not. I did not go on the trip and Father Bob had no idea. I decided to talk with the whole group of students at one time and make my decision after our conversation. I proceeded to call the students down into the activity center/library at around 11:00 a.m. This would give the students time to think about the entire situation. If I knew anything at all, I knew students seem to always tell the truth without their parents around. They change their stories once the parents get involved. I think parental pressure is not always a positive move. Lying is something that is taught, as one gets older. People are not born to lie but most people take it for granted because the majority of people do it and never give it a second thought.

I have always tried to tell the truth no matter what the cost. It has helped me keep my self-respect because that is one thing only I can give away. Keeping my self-respect and being honest are two things I hold dearly in my heart. My life would be meaningless if I gave these away.

I started the meeting with a short prayer and proceeded to talk about the trip itself. I reminded the students about the trip being school sponsored because of School Board action. The three-day suspension was never an issue with the students. They knew what I had to do and accepted it. Again, the problem was trying to figure out who was guilty and who was not. I told the students I was not the Lord and they would have to step up and take their punishment. What I didn't want was to punish someone who was innocent. I remember one student saying I wanted the students to rat on each other. This was one thing students will never do no matter what the cost. I explained I did not see it that way. I explained it was time to do the right thing but I needed their help. The students knew me for a long time and knew what I stood for long before this situation took place. One student stood up at this point and stated he did not drink. Another student said he might not have drunk but he purchased his for him. I could see the students caught on to what I wanted them to do. At this point, I decided to let the students handle the situation. I gave them a little better than one hour and they brought me a list. Sixty-three students admitted they were guilty and the remainder were innocent. I went downstairs and thanked the students for being honest even though they knew what it meant. I told the 63 they would get the next three days off and Father Bob and I would be working something out that would involve their parents. The 63 remained in school for the rest of the day while I called their parents. Most parents knew what was coming and did not disagree with what I had to do.

Later that same afternoon Father Bob and I decided to write their parents a letter saying that we scheduled a mandatory meeting in the church for Thursday night in which all 63 students and parents had to attend if their children were coming back on Friday morning. We stated that we were going to have speakers talk with them but the ski trip itself would not be discussed. It was done and over. We both signed the letter and they were sent out that same afternoon.

The student and parent meeting went well and everything seemed to be working out until Father Bob decided to take the stand after our speakers were finished. He opened the meeting for discussion and went back to the trip itself. I was sitting in the back of the church at the time and knew what was coming. One parent raised his hand and Father Bob called on him. I could see this parent was blasted when he could hardly stand up without holding onto the pew. Instead of Father Bob not discussing the trip like the letter said, he chose to respond to his questions. Father Bob finally found himself in a situation he could not win. So what did he do? He stated that I was the principal and everything was up to me. I stood up and read the part of the letter that stated that the trip itself would not be discussed. I also told the parents if they wanted to discuss the trip itself I would be in my office in the morning and I would be willing to talk about the situation. On Friday morning, no parent showed up to discuss the matter at hand.

The parent that wanted to discuss the trip on Thursday night went to the office of the Superintendent of Catholic Schools in Saginaw, Dr. John Morris, to complain. Dr. Morris called me later and took the side of the angry parent. He thought by not allowing those 63 students to go on a school sponsored ski trip again was enough punishment. I told him no further school sponsored ski trips were or would be scheduled and the three days suspensions would hold. Needless to say, Dr. Morris and I did not see eye to eye on this matter and/or things coming down the road.

Chapter III

A NEW HIGH SCHOOL

SAGINAW NOUVEL

I was having lunch with Bishop Kenneth Ulander while we were at a teacher conference in Saginaw, Michigan. He was in attendance to celebrate the mass with the staffs of St. Stephen Parish High School, Sts. Peter and Paul High School and St. Mary's High School. The topic of the day was "Social Justice" and the Bishop was a great speaker who could inspire anyone. He was a PR man all the way and loved by most of the people who met him. I mentioned that now would be a good time to consolidate the three Catholic High Schools because they were all having financial problems and it was looking like one or two of the three could close. He agreed and that was actually the end of our conversation on the topic.

Monday morning rolled around and Dr. John Morris was in my office. Before I could say a word, he let me know that the Bishop decided to move on my suggestion. I asked him what that was. He explained that the Bishop agreed with me and is going to run with my idea of combining the three high schools and forming a new one. I told him that was great and we continued to talk. He told me the Bishop wanted the new school to start in the fall of that year and things had to be done yesterday.

I remember thinking that this move would be to fast. I understood why he wanted the new high school to start as soon as possible. By doing it now he would cut down on all the opposition he would be getting. People are usually conservative in their thoughts and actions and are against change in any way. This would be a drastic change in the Saginaw Diocese and people felt comfortable having their own school in their neighborhood. They feel more of a part of it when they can see it and have invested their time and money in trying to keep the dying horse alive at any cost. John said he would be getting back to me as well as the other two principals and clergy as soon as he could. He said I would be free to let everyone know and things would begin to happen.

I spread the word to my staff knowing they would tell the students and they would inform their parents. Most people I talked to were not against the idea but wanted all their questions answered now. My staff was concerned about their jobs. The students and parents wanted to know the building's location seeing we had three different campuses in different locations around the Saginaw Area.

Many other concerns came to the forefront, as the summer break was about to begin. The Bishop took little time in putting Dr. Morris and his staff in charge setting up meetings about every day and night of the week. I was asked to serve on the financial committee trying to set up what it would cost.

I was really impressed with the finance committee and was proud to be part of it. The committee met and chose Hugh LeFrost, a local attorney, as the chairman. We met for over a month and brought our recommendations to the Bishop. Later that week each committee member received a letter stating thanks but no thanks and the committee was dissolved by the Bishop. Boy, was I upset. It seemed like the Bishop had a financial plan in mind before we even met. My guess was our plan did not fit with what he wanted. We wanted all students to pay their share even though we knew we might be losing students along the way. Students will be lost when new things are tried just because it's an excuse to pull out and not face the financial burden it might cost. Many parents were strapped for money and an increase in tuition was just too much to take.

I knew the committee wasn't recommending what the Bishop wanted but disbanding the committee the way he did made my intentions clear. We felt like we wasted our time and things began to fall apart. Word spread and the wide spread support that the Bishop had was fading away. Panic began to set in and things fell apart overnight. The new high school would still be opened in the Fall because this was what the Bishop wanted. He had the type of personality that would not allow him to listen and/or be told he was wrong on any matter being discussed. His agenda was his and that was that. I could hear Father Bob saying the same even though he was now in Bay City as the Pastor of St. Boniface Parish and not taking an active role in forming the new high school. I lived in Bay City at the time and belonged to Visitation Parish. This was a blessing in my eyes but I could hear the echoes coming. I knew Father Bob was involved just by the tone coming from the Bishop. They both had the same type of personality that turned me off.

They could not be questioned about anything and could not live with criticism of any type. They both felt like they were speaking for the Lord himself by doing things in the name of Jesus. I realized early when they gave that response they were being questioned and they could not stand it.

Things kept moving along forming the new high school that was scheduled to open in the Fall. Anxiety was starting to set in, as the new building picked was Sts. Peter and Paul High School. It was the best location, as the population seemed to be moving into Saginaw Township. St Stephen still had its grade school while St. Mary's was in bad shape. This building would now house the Central Office for the Saginaw Diocese, the Bishop's Offices and the new high school. But, the teaching staffs were now very concerned about having a job in the Fall. Combining three staffs into one with most likely a smaller enrollment to begin with, would dictate a smaller teaching staff. Who was going to be hired and when would this be taking place?

The superintendent, Dr. John Morris, seemed to be the only one who had a clue. Just before the current school year was coming to an end, he called a meeting between the three staffs to answer their concerns. The meeting was held at St. Mary's High School. John started the meeting with a pep talk about what was going on with the new school that lasted for most of the meeting. He did not touch on any of the real concerns of the three staffs and stated that an administrator would have to be hired first. Once this was done, a staff could be hired shortly thereafter. This seemed to be the logical thing to do at that time.

Everything was going very smoothly until I asked him about the rumors that were spreading. I heard he had been out to California and offered the position of principal to a nun. He had three principals he could just about choose

---

from and went out and picked an outsider even though the three of us had worked out a plan so nobody would be left out. Of course he denied the whole rumor and stated it was not true. I wanted to believe him but I knew better. I had heard this from a very reliable source at this central office and knew he was lying. The meeting broke for mass to be followed by a short luncheon. In the meantime, John called all three administrators into an office. He actually lost his cool and told me never to put him on the spot like I had done. I knew he and I didn't see eye to eye but this actually nailed the coffin on me applying for any position at the new high school. I could not work for a man who could and/or would not tell the truth and expect me to respect him. About a week later, the new principal from California was announced. I had nothing against her at this point and looked forward to meeting her.

I had worked for Sr. Anne Olog as her assistant for four years at St. Stephens. She taught me a lot about being a secondary administrator. She had it her way and always said if anyone disagreed with her she would be gone because she had a very competent assistant who could take over the next day. This person was yours truly. She and I were very close and worked well together.

The principal arrived about a week later and came to my office. I could see right away that she was no Sr. Anne. She had new ideas that were out of sight and I knew I didn't belong. She was a little upset I did not apply and would not be going to the new school. Later she met my teaching staff one at a time for a short interview before selecting her staff. I chose to apply at Bay City All Saints for a principal position that just opened. Things had changed so much at St. Stephen's I knew it was time for me to say goodbye.

I liked their new pastor, Father John Roester but he had his problems. Once Bishop Ulander sent him away to dry out and John came right back. Bishop Ulander could never say no to priests who fought him. He needed every priest he could get to cover the many different parishes.

After working with so many different priests during my years at St Stephen's Parish, Father John Roester and Father Henry Ducharles were actually the only ones I respected. I did not always agree with them but they earned my respect. There were many associate Pastors who were in another world. These associate pastors for the most part wanted the Pope to allow priests to marry. Most priests usually had a friend who traveled whenever the priest changed to a different parish. Many had a girl friend because they were only human. I usually graded them below the average person once I got to know them better. I worked with priests and nuns who were alcoholics, went on personal vacations without wearing their collars and swore and lied as much as anyone I could think of. I once brought my mother to the Saginaw Downs and introduced her to one of the associate pastors at St. Stephen's Parish at the time and she could not believe what she saw and heard. My mother was old schooled in the Catholic System in Cheboygan, Michigan. She raised her five children catholic while my father was Lutheran. My father was not tied into his church and their marriage lasted for only nineteen years. I do not believe religion had anything to do with their divorce but having two religions in one family didn't seem to help matters.

The associate pastor was swearing like a mule. He was out of control and using the F word more times than I could count. He was not wearing his white collar and I was hoping people did not recognize him. When he had the morning mass with the elementary children he would ask me what the F___ are we having mass about today. People at mass would never know what I knew about this priest. I believe I was starting to lose my faith in the Catholic Church with its leaders around this time. Remember what I knew about Father Bob. My thought was that many of them were hypocrites and should not be living and doing what they preached against. The Catholic Church believes priests have the power to forgive your sins if your confession was sincere. I thought how could people like the ones I have mentioned have this power given to them by the Lord?

Needless to say, I do not believe priests have this power. Lately, I wonder if I should join another religion? Maybe I knew too much and I would be better off not knowing. As Principal, I was responsible for everything the Pre-School-Grade 12 system had going. I scheduled a Christmas Party for the entire staff each and every year. Once I scheduled it in the convent that was built for around thirty sisters. It was a great location and I had everything delivered and put into the huge refrigerator about a week before the event. I decided to check things out and get ready for the evening party by going to the convent early. It was a good thing I did. When I opened the refrigerator, it was empty. The nuns had taken everything. They decided to help themselves and take everything home for the holidays. I was in shock to say the least. We only had four nuns living in the convent at the time. We had enough for over one hundred guests. I quickly went shopping and the party went off as planned.

I remember Father Henry P. Ducharles coming to my office one morning. I could see he was really upset. He told me the four nuns were driving him crazy. They were from two different orders and could not get along. They shared one car and fought over its usage all the time. Getting another car was out of the question. He said two would have to go. I had to pick between the younger or older ones. I chose the older nuns and the younger ones had to go.

People might think that nuns were cheaper to hire than a layman or woman. This was not the case. The nuns had additional expenses laypeople did not have and the church was not responsible for such things as a vehicle. If a nun was hired, with people and nuns living longer, the church had to pay for one additional retired nun along with the one working. I know of many elementary catholic schools actually paid one-half of what their contract said they made. The other half was a donation to the Church. I thought this was wrong but these laypeople were not given a choice. That's the way things were done at the time so parishes could meet their budgets. I worked with around a two million dollar yearly budget at St. Stephens while I was principal. I knew from past experience this amount put a heavy burden on the parish and I could not ever go over budget and I never did. Mr. Richard Dowdrey was a principal at St. Stephens before me. I was his assistant principal for three years. Richard did everything he could for the students over this period of time. His only mistake was going over the budget one time and he chose to leave. Years later, I hired him back as a science teacher and he did an outstanding job. Sister Anne followed Mr. Dowdrey as I became her assistant for the next four years. She left to become a lawyer for her order and I became principal shortly thereafter. She had her ways but I learned more from her than anyone. Her belief was she had four years to bend and mode starting teachers while she left teachers with more than four years experience alone unless they needed her help. She knew her stuff even though many students and parents didn't care for her ways of doing things.

As the new school, Nouvel Catholic High School, was taking shape, I received a call from the business manager of Sts. Peter and Paul Area High School. He asked me to see him about the Principal of his school. I drove out that afternoon to see what he wanted me to know about. The decision on who would be the principal of Nouvel was not made public yet and he thought I would be the one. He did not know I was not going to apply and I had already taken another Principal position in Bay City. He proceeded to tell me that the principal of Sts. Peter and Paul had been taking large amounts of money from the school. He was ordering new textbooks and making a double order. One order was in his name. When he sent the order in his name back to the company, he had the money credited to his personal account. This was unbelievable and totally dishonest. The business manager wanted to know what he should do. I told him I would let Bishop Ulander know about this situation as soon as possible. With the new school being formed, the Bishop didn't want the public to find out. The Bishop chose to let him go without any criminal charges and get him and his family counseling. Around the same time, the same principal was caught taking pictures of the boys while they were taking showers. These two things could only damage what the Bishop had put together pertaining to Nouvel. He was not going to make the information public and chose to ignore the situation for the most part. What else could he do? The new high school was off to a shaky start. The new principal had ideas I knew would never fly. She wanted to make her teaching staff all counselors for the students. The teachers knew this along with their other responsibilities would never work. But, they had no choice in the matter. The new principal only lasted for one year and she left Nouvel and the area.

CHAPTER IV

FOR BETTER OR WORST

A NEW BEGINNING

I was now under contract for one year to be the principal of Bay City All Saints. I was now going to have an assistant principal and athletic director, two campuses and eight feeder elementary catholic schools. I had friends who worked at All Saints and seemed to like it very much. It was going to be different than St. Stephens for the first fourteen years of my career. I was looking forward to not only working in Bay City, I also lived there. I would no longer have to make that trip from Bay City to Saginaw at least ten times a week. I felt more at home from the very beginning. My contract would start on the first of July and I was prepared and ready for new challenges in my life.

I woke up one morning in June of same year and my lawn was driven through the night before. I had no idea as to who might have done the damage but I was going to find out. I finally got the word before the week was up. They were All Saints students who wanted to get a certain teacher and added me to their list without ever knowing me and just because I was going to be their new principal. I called one of the boy's fathers and he took care of the damage along with the teacher's yard within a few days. I asked myself what had I gotten myself into because nothing like this had ever happened before. But, I shook it off and let it go.

I arrived on All Saints north campus on the morning of July 1st. and got the surprise of my life. Bishop Ken Ulander was on the phone and wanted to talk to me. He said the only priest interested in becoming pastor of All Saints was Father Bob DeLong. He knew we did not see eye to eye and wondered if I could give it another try. I was a great public relations person and told him I could work with anyone. Bob would be a challenge but I was hoping he had grown up after leaving St. Stephens Parish. I told the Bishop I would do it for him and he said thanks.

I could hear the echoes running down the hall outside my office and I could see the Reverend Robert DeLong coming. We sat and talked for some time without a mention of the many times he set me up while trying to look like he knew what he was doing and never taking the blame. But, it wasn't long into our conversation when things started to change from bad to worse.

I took the All Saints job knowing I had an assistant principal, athletic director and two campuses. I was told everything was ready for the coming school year. Boy, this was all as far from the truth as one could get. There was no plan and nothing was done for next year. I could not believe what I was hearing. The school was in a chaotic state of anarchy. It was a mess. The principal who left did absolutely nothing because she knew she was not coming back. Enrollment was not taken and no master schedule was put together. Teachers were not given contracts while textbooks and teaching materials were never ordered. I knew it was going to be a long year. I had to make a decision. I could roll up my sleeves and start over or walk out. I decided to give it my best shot.

The first thing I had to do was find out who was coming to All Saints in the Fall. From that I could build a schedule and hire a staff along with textbooks and teaching materials. The textbooks were so old and in such bad shape, they had to be replaced. Why should any parent spend the money it was going to cost to send their children to All Saints if they knew what I was finding out? I called in two secretaries and the three of us started making calls to parents and parishes letting them know we would be there for next year. I guess it was a good way of meeting the parents and students on an individual basis. I found out a lot of parents were upset with the school for previous decisions made and chose not to come back. All Saints was a lot different than St. Stephens in Saginaw. St. Stephen students came from homes of professional people. Bay City All Saints was made up of a lot of blue-collar parents in an economy heading the wrong way. Times were bad and getting worse.

The previous principal had fired the basketball coach, Mr. Lefty Franz, and he was a legion in his own time. Later in his career he would be voted into the Michigan Coaches Hall of Fame. Lefty was a good friend and I had known him and his family for many years. His older brother Sam, another Hall of Fame Coach, worked at St. Stephen as the head basketball coach for nine years before. We were great buddies. This was a great mistake made by the previous administration. So, I decided to ask Lefty if he wanted to return. He said he would be doing to another what was done to him and he said he could not do it. No matter how much I begged I received the same answer. I knew what he was saying and believed in what he stood for. My respect for this man could not be any higher. Lefty was a member of St. Stan's Parish and it was the biggest feeder elementary Catholic school in all of Bay City. All Saints would not be there if it wasn't for this parish. Lefty stayed at All Saints as a Government teacher and we went on from there. I even tried to get Lefty's wife to come back and teach but she said she was tired and could not do it at this time.

The master schedule was finally put together after we knew more about who was coming to All Saints or not. The enrollment numbers had dropped off tremendously for many more reasons than the ones stated above. The school was now going to be a small Class D high school scheduled to play A & B schools in athletics for the next two years. Athletic contracts were signed for a two-year period of time and it would take at least this amount of time to contract smaller and more competitive schools in the future. This was just another mistake made in the past. Enrollment seemed to go up and down according to a school's win and lost record for most Catholic High Schools in the State. Parents did not want to pay the extra money if the school was losing. They wanted to send their children to a winning school and not one losing most contests. I knew this would hurt All Saints for at least the next two years because of the signed contracts. I was right and for the next two years the varsity football team never won a contest. The team seemed to play even up for the first half of the games and then things fell apart. The school had to many guys playing both ways along with playing larger schools. Enrollment kept going down at the feeder elementary schools and this had the same effect on All Saints.

One of the first things I did was schedule a meeting with the priest at the North and South campus. Father Lauer at St. James campus or North campus and I had a down to earth talk about the future of All Saints as he saw it. He did ask me what I thought about Bishop Ken Ulander taking so long to bring his girl friend to the area. I met her on two different occasions but pretended I did not know what he was talking about and he filled me in on the details. When Father Ken was made a bishop one of the first things he did was to move out of the rectory. His excuse was it would give him a chance to visit and live at the parishes in his diocese.

I remember when he lived at St. Stephen Parish he was hardly there. I wondered where he was. My guess was he was no better than anyone else. He had needs and he saw to it they were met. This was just another reason I do not hold people up to a higher standard because they will most likely fall from grace. Priests are only human no matter what people think.

When the numbers for All Saints finally came in my next visit was to meet with the priest at south campus. I knew at this point I had to consolidate the school at one campus and North made more sense. Four teachers and my assistant principal and athletic director had to be let go. This was not the way I wanted to start. To meet the budget it had to be done. One member of the school board represented Holy Trinity Parish and his son in law was one I had to let go. He was also going to be my athletic director and assistant principal and now I would have to do it all. I had done it before but I felt like I should walk out because the Board was not honest in representing the state of the school during my interview. I knew most school boards don't really know much. Board members usually have a private agenda and once their item is over they resign and/or choose not to run again. Personally, I believe local school boards should be done away with. Regional boards would make more sense by allowing administrators to run the operation of the district without playing politics. It's nice to have local control but let's face the facts. It's a game of popularity and that's it. It would be like me serving on the decision making body of a hospital or corporation I did not understand. What a joke.

I decided to stay and try my best making All Saints a winner in all respects. I met with members of the Board and Father DeLong and told them what had to be done. I explained I would do everything but I had to have a full time secretary for the athletic area. They went along and I pulled up my sleeves and began. I found out All Saints Athletic Program was spread out among the feeder parishes. St. Joe's Elementary housed most of the inventory while the football equipment was located at St. Stan's Elementary School because All Saints did not have a gym. Things started to take shape after an inventory was taken, lights had to be wired at St. Joe along with a new P.A. System installed. The baseball and softball fields were located in another part of town owned by the Knights of Columbus on River Road. Things were finally pieced together and we seemed to be ready for another year.

The first thing I wanted to do was to meet the students. I decided to set up a dance at St. Hyacinth's gymnasium when school started. I thought this would give me a good chance to know them and they could meet me in a setting other than the school. It turned out to be a bad idea but I got my message across.

The dance started out on a positive note. The students and I were eager to get to know each other. About midway through the dance I decided to take a walk outside. I met the two policemen I hired for the night. They were actual policemen who worked the dances for the extra money. Once the students were inside the dance they could not leave unless they were leaving for the night. This rule stops a lot of problems before they begin. I noticed the students left quite a few cars wide open. It was a hot night and many of the windows were also open. I started to notice cases of beer and brown bags of alcohol inside the cars. I called the police over and asked them what this was. They told me this was the way it was at All Saints. They said that the students never drink before the dance but usually have a party after. I said this would be the end of it and had the police pick up and stack in the gymnasium all the alcohol they could see. The students were all under age and they all could be facing a minor in possession charge. I could not believe what I was seeing.

The police found around twenty-five cases and fifteen bottles of hard stuff from the cars and trucks in the parking lot. This was not counting what was in the trunks. I told the students what I was doing and if they wanted to get their alcohol they could face charges. Not one student asked. When the dance ended I told the two policemen to take the alcohol when they left. They agreed and left the dance. I knew if I chose to search the trunks the two policemen would have to get warrants for each vehicle and they really did not want to do it. I made my point and alcohol was never a problem again at one of the dances.

The following Monday morning I saw Father Bob coming down the hall. He said two parents were interested in bringing an exchange student from Germany to All Saints for the rest of the year. I was all for schools taking exchange students. I had two criteria they had to meet. I wanted them to take classes counting towards their graduation back in their home country. I did not want the students who already graduated high school back home because they were only here for one purpose. I had taken one from South America at St. Stephens and he had to be sent back for smoking and drinking. He told me he was only here to party and see what the United States was like. Father Bob said he would agree with my two demands. He would make the contact with the parents. He later stated the young man was a great skier and he would like to have a skiing team at All Saints. He was willing to coach the team for free because he loved to ski himself. I knew where this was all going from the very beginning but I agreed because I was trying to work with Bob.

I met the American parents with Father Bob when the exchange student from Germany arrived. I realized from our discussion the young man had already moved beyond high school in Germany and he was here to party. I was disappointed in Father Bob again because he was trying to get to involved with the students and didn't seem to care about what we agreed to. It was to late to change things and we moved on. It did not take long to form the ski team even though we would now have to travel about two hours North in order to have a meet. The team had to practice in Freeland at Apple Mountain Ski Resort that wasn't that challenging to begin with. The real resorts with competitive slopes were all up north. Soon after we had everything in place things started to fall apart. Our exchange student was so bad he never made it down our practice hill in Freeland let alone at any competitive event. His American parents wanted to send him back to Germany because he was smoking and drinking way too much. Finally, Father Bob told him he could stay at his rectory under his supervision but had to follow his rules. It wasn't long and Bob sent him back to Germany because of his behavior. Needless to say, the ski team was doomed and Father Bob took it on the chin.

The rest of my first year at All Saints went well. Things were coming together and the school was finally pulling in the right direction. I noticed the area public schools had weighted grades which gave extra honor points for students taking the harder college prep courses. The staff was in favor of adopting this system and developed courses to fit the criteria. It was something new and the students and parents were all in favor. It would start in the Fall of the following year.

This was actually the little item that would lead me into the public school system and away from Board approval on any item coming up. During the summer of the year (1985) a parent and her daughter scheduled a meeting with me to discuss weighted grades and the courses developed by the staff. Her husband was on the Board and wanted me to change the honor points for a Creative Writing course her daughter received two years before because in was called the same name. It would move her to number two in her class barely in front of the girl who had that position. I told her I never changed a grade for any student and I was not about to start with her daughter. I knew what this could mean but I stood firm.

I believe the Board for the most part wanted me to make the change but I refused. I had to stand by my principles and what I believed in no matter what the cost. My self-respect means more to me than just about anything. It is something I had to live with the rest of my life and it could not be taken away without my approval. It was not going to happen and I could still look in the mirror and be proud of what was starring back. My good relationship with the Board changed from this day on. I was no longer invited to the Hub Bar with Board members after our monthly meetings and I knew the Echo was in the air. Board members started voting against my wishes and I could see the writing on the walls. But before the above event took place the Board along with Father Bob offered me a three-year contract I accepted as principal and athletic director. At this point I could do no wrong. The small additional amount I was going to get for being the athletic director was to this day never paid to me. It was only $2,500 more per year for three years. I never wanted to be the school's athletic director anyway along with all my other responsibilities I had to do. Someone had to do it and I agreed. I thought the issue was over after I signed the multi-year contract but I was wrong. Father Bob was about to stir up more trouble than he wanted or could handle. In the meantime a friend of mine Dr. Michael Burowski the principal of Holy Trinity stopped in my office. We had a long talk as he explained his problem to me and what he was going to do about it. He said there was a family at his parish elementary school and they wanted him out. He was very concerned they were going to do whatever they could to get him. He told me his plan and I told him not to bother. The clergy was against him including Father Bob. I never knew why but he was talking about some car being parked outside his home over the last few nights.

He said he had scheduled an appointment with Bishop Ken Ulander and he had something on him and wanted his support. I told him the Bishop would never go against his priests and everyone already knew about the Bishop's friend. He said he was going to make sure everyone knew about the Bishop's relationship and he was going to get word out to the general public. I told him it was not going to change anything and forget about it. We agreed to talk about what happened after his meeting with the Bishop the next day. But, the next day never came for Mike. He kept his meeting with the Bishop and disappeared shortly thereafter. I wondered what had happened? A policeman from the Bay City office came to my office a few days later because he knew I was one of the last people Mike had talked to before he met with the Bishop. He was now a missing person and the police had very little to go on. I told the policeman about our conversation and he left. I never saw him again.

About ten years later Mike's body was found in the local river. It was amazing but after this long a period of time his body was in good shape except for his head. His head was detached from his frame and nobody seemed to know why. Who was at fault? The police finally called it a homicide and the issue was over. Too many years had passed and the police had little to nothing to carry out their investigation any further. Mike's file was closed and it has bothered me ever since. Was it a suicide and why was his head still in his car and separated from the rest of his body? I guess I'll never know.

Chapter V

COVERING

MINI-MICRO RECORDER

Father Bob was coming down the corridor and I could tell something was up and my mistrust of him led me to tape our conversation for my protection. We worked very well together for one year but I knew the honeymoon was over. He had a little smile on his face when he entered. He did not know my mini-micro recorder was on and placed inside my desk with the drawer open. It would pick up any conversation we were having. I felt guilty for doing what had to be done and I had no other choice. I carried this recorder from that day on in my suit coat just in case. I know using it was not legal without the other person's knowledge but I had to do what I had to do. My trust of Father Bob left me with no other choice.

He started his conversation off by stating the Bay City Parochial System with All Saints and all the feeder elementary schools were being put together with one leader for Vicariate VIII. He said I could apply and I would be considered. I asked him about my recently signed three-year contract as Principal of All Saints and he said it would be considered in the selection process. All the Catholic Schools in the area were having financial hardships and some changes had to be made. I told him he had to do what he had to do. I would do likewise. I was always good at reading between the lines and knew with the recent change of events he was not looking at me to fill this new position. I told him I would think about it and he left for the day. I shut off my recorder and went on doing my daily duties.

The next thing I realized was Father Bob talking about interviewing Mr. Jeff Wisel as a possible Athletic Director for next year. Jeff was a parent who had been thinking about retirement from his job but could not make up his mind. I set up the interview with Jeff a few days later. Jeff was a caring individual who had sent his children to All Saints and was well known in the community and well respected by others and myself. The interview went great and I was so happy someone was interested in taking over the AD job I really had no time to do along with my other responsibilities. The more we talked it seemed like Jeff could not decide what he wanted to do. I offered him the job and he said he would have to think about it. I said fine and please let me know what you decide.

The school board monthly meeting was held about a week later. I had not heard a word from Jeff at this point. I could only assume he was not interested. I was sitting in the board room when I saw Father Bob coming in with Jeff. I knew what was about to happen and I was right on. Bob introduced Jeff as the next Athletic Director for All Saints without ever contacting me. I could see the writing on the wall. I thought I should have been contacted either by Jeff and/or Father Bob before the meeting. That did not happen. Bob had worked things out with Jeff without my knowledge so he could look good to the board. He actually nailed the coffin shut on my three year contract by changing it without my input in the decision making process. The sad part was he thought he was taking over and I would just go along with whatever he said. When he stated he does things in the name of the lord is a key in not trusting what he is about to say. I do not believe the lord ever talked to Father Bob let alone tell him what he must do. He uses this as a way of trying to get his way without question. I must admit I do not believe any priest has the power to forgive sins. My experience has told me priests commit as much sin as anyone else. Sometimes I wonder how they can look in the mirror if you know what I mean. I have seen many preach one thing and live a different life. I know they are not perfect but this has to be a joke. Many priests should actually leave the priesthood because they are doing more wrong than right. The damage they have done is not worth the price. They are not experts in everything and should stick to what they know. Most pastors have a parish with a school yet the priests have very little background in elementary and/or secondary education. But like Bob they try to run the show. Many times they tend to do more harm than good for their own sake while creating problems for others. It seems the more Bob got involved in school matters the more harm came about.

Father Bob came in one morning to talk to the seniors. He did not tell me what he wanted to say but scheduled himself into their classes. I was a little surprised at this move but I had no choice in the matter because I was still trying to get along with him. All of a sudden I noticed a funny noise coming from the halls on the third floor. This is where Bob was meeting with the seniors. Word spread to me Bob ended up stretching the truth a bit. The seniors asked him what was happening with my job and he told them I was willing to do whatever he said.

I actually said he must do what he had to while I'll do what I have to do. This was a far cry from what he was saying to the seniors. I had only been at All Saints for a year and one-half and was totally surprised at the senior's next move. They decided to walk out on him and went into the parking lot to protest. Bob tried to get them back but they refused. He finally came to my office and demanded me to get them back into class. I told him he should not lie and telling them the truth would have been a lot better. At this point the entire student body was out in the parking lot. Students are very honest for the most part. They seem to stretch the truth once their parents get involved. But that was not the case. Father Bob was caught in another lie and the students were calling him out on it.

I finally decided to go out into the parking lot to see what I could do about the situation. I knew who was leading the walkout and he and I talked. The student body finally decided to go back into their classes after I asked them. Father Bob had lost their respect for lying to them but they trusted me and knew I really cared about them. I have always believed if the students know you really care about them they will back you 150 percent. The trust is usually there because of one's position. To care is the real key. For the most part students truly need someone who cares in our mixed up society we live in. Students seem to always be on the up and up. They will always give you their support as long as you have gained their respect by being honest and showing them you truly care. They can see through a fake without batting an eye.

Towards the end of my second year and two more years on my contract I knew what I had to do. I decided to sue the Bishop because he was actually the official leader of the Catholic Schools in the Saginaw Diocese included the Bay City Parochial System. This was one of the hardest decisions I ever had to make. Bishop Ken Ulander was a friend and I could only guess what he was thinking. I actually was left with no other choice. Father Bob did not want to honor my contract and our means of communication once I would not change a students grade came to an end. I had to look for another job because my oldest son was now about to attend college and bills had to be paid. Father Bob told me he would not give me a recommendation if I chose to sue. I felt at a certain point in one's life a critical decision has to be made. This was that time in mine. I only wish I would have done it many years before.

I left All Saints in much better shape than when I found her. The master schedule was finished for the following year. Enrollment numbers were taken and teaching supplies were ordered. Athletic schedules were set with their teams playing more competitive schools in their own division. Everything was in place and I felt good about the job I had done. They still owed me for being the Athletic Director for the past two years. I did receive a call from one of my secretaries. She told me the new principal they hired changed the grade and the girl became number two in next year's senior class. I felt like a new person when I left and the echo might finally be gone forever.

As things turned out, I did not need a recommendation from Father Bob and I signed a new two-year contract in northern Michigan shortly thereafter. I did realize contracts are usually not worth the paper they are written on. Things can change overnight like they have in my case. My self-respect was still in tack and life was good again.

The one thing I lost in working for the Catholic System was my faith in the church because of the individuals trying to control it. I have not attended church since I left All Saints. How can I respect the church and the individuals running the show with everything I knew? I am still a God fearing man who talks to the Lord each and every day. That will never change. This might sound a little nuts but I believe on one day I saw the Holy Spirit. It appeared and was gone before I knew what it was until I thought about what happened. It was a beautiful sight I will never forget. If it was the Holy Spirit or not it doesn't matter. I believe what I believe.

In case you are wondering about my lawsuit against Bishop Ulander I finally sent him a copy of my tape recording I made when I had my conversation with Father Bob. I received a call within a few days from the Bishop and he wanted to settle. The Bishop was a good friend for quite some time. It's hard to sue a friend even though he owed me in the six-figure area plus benefits. I decided to settle for the amount it cost me in getting another job. I cannot tell anyone the exact amount but it was a small amount. How can you sue a friend who is the Bishop? We parted as friends and it was settled out of court.

I truly wanted to sue Father Bob but that never materialized. So, the issue was over a few weeks after I took another job.

Chapter VI

THIS MAKES NUMBER THREE

THREE AND OUT

I interviewed for a principal's position within the Manistee Nation Forest Area next and was offered the position. The superintendent and I met at the Dority Hotel in Clare, Michigan and I signed the contract. I returned home with the good news and within a few minutes I received another call from Mr. Claude Foot the Superintendent of Standish-Sterling Community Schools wanting to know if I was interested in coming to Standish, Michigan. I told him I would have to call him back because I had just signed a two-year contract with another school district. I told him I would be interested in Standish because it wasn't as far north as the other district and it was the school district my wife, Gloria J. (Michalik) Haut was from. We owned land in the Standish District and knew the area well. I called the superintendent in the Manistee area and he told me to interview. I was surprised and then he told me he was also looking for another job. He wished me good luck and he would be waiting to here from me ASAP. I said thanks and I took the interview at Standish-Sterling the next night.

Mr. Foot called me after the interview and offered me the position if I could get out of the contract I signed the day before. I called the superintendent and he was happy for me. He said he hated to lose me because I had done everything he was looking for in his position while I was with the Catholic Schools. I thanked him and wished him the best in looking for another position himself.

I felt great and was looking forward to working for Mr. Foot and the Standish-Sterling Community School District. Mr. Foot and I hit it off right from the start. He had gone to Parochial schools his entire life and had a good idea of what I had done over the sixteen years I spent working for them. I never made any real money but that was not what I wanted out of my life. My retirement after working for sixteen years and being one of the highest paid administrators in the Parochial System would only amount to $275.00 a month when I had to retire in 2004. The Catholic System was actually set up for nuns and priests with a home and no expenses. Like I said before I should have never taken the job in this system in the first place. This was my choice and I can only blame myself. I did find out more than half of my staff at All Saints quit shortly after I left. I must admit I was a little spoiled from the two schools I was at. I started at St Stephen's and came up to principal in a short period of time. Because I was one of them, the staff and I had a great relationship to say the least. At All Saints the staff and I came together as one just about over night. I told them everything going on with the schools and what I thought the future would be like for All Saints and the feeder elementary schools. I was sorry to hear about what was happening at All Saints with the staff but it actually worked out to their advantage financially. They could hire cheaper teachers and save a few dollars. I hoped everything went well for them and their school and knew I was never coming back.

Standish-Sterling Community Schools is a small Class B school district and extremely conservative in its' thinking. Things have stayed the same for a number of years. The master schedule had been the same for far to many years. The computer system was so obsolete the ones they had would not make a good typewriter. My secretary told me if I ever changed to using computers she would retire. She thought she was too old to change and didn't need it. Textbooks were so old in the junior and Senior Highs man had not landed on the moon yet. This was the actual truth of the matter. Many teachers taught the way they were taught thirty years before with the same books. The English Department taught out of what they called the great books and fought any change what-so-ever. Like the movie called "The Teacher" they actually had teachers use the same book and student handouts for more than thirty years. Students would do handout after handout without ever talking to the teacher on a regular basis. I believe teachers could have died at their desk and the students wouldn't know it until school was out for the day. I truly believed the staff was set in their ways and never wanted to change anything. It did not take me long to know this school needed more attention than the two parochial schools I had been to years before. Standish-Sterling was a consolidated school district and thirty years later there were still hard feelings in both communities about consolidation. I could not say Standish without saying Sterling immediately after. Everyone seemed to be related to everyone. It actually didn't take long for word to get around on any subject. I always thought this was a big disadvantage for the district. Time seemed to be standing still for the community and the school district itself. What was good for the parents seemed to be as good for their children. I felt like something had to be done to help prepare the students for their future outside of the Standish-Sterling area. This would become a constant battle for the eighteen years I would spend in the district. At least the new Superintendent, Mr. Claude L. Foot, and I would agree on this matter.

SUPER'S CONFERENCE

The honeymoon did not last long when I realized what was happening after a short period of time. The echo was returning harder than the other two put together and lasting much longer. Claude, the Superintendent, asked me to go with him to a superintendent's conference in Grand Rapids, Michigan. I told him I really did not want to go because I would feel out of place not being a superintendent myself. He said he really wanted me to go and who knows it might pay off for me in the future. He knew I always wanted to be a superintendent of schools so I finally agreed. The day came and I was ready to go. Claude was running late for some reason and we finally left Standish about one hour after our planned time of departure. I knew we were going to be there for two days and I could not figure out why Claude was in such a rush.

Claude drove his little Pontiac that was his two-seat sports car. It could really travel. We took M-61 through Gladwin at a very high rate of speed. I kept looking for the fire and asked him to slow down before he killed someone. He was finally pulled over for speeding just outside of Gladwin. I thought thank God. This might slow him down a bit. But as luck would have it the under sheriff was a graduate of Standish- Sterling and knew both of us. He gave Mr. Foot a warning and let him go without a ticket. We hit M-127 and Mr. Foot was off to the races again. This time he buried the odometer at 120 miles an hour. I finally said what the hell are you doing. He cut his speed down to around 80-85 mph for the rest of the trip. He said he was running late for an appointment and was in a hurry to get there. I had no idea of what he was talking about but knew he was running his own agenda. Out of the clear blue sky he said this will be like Las Vegas. What happens in Grand Rapids stays in Grand Rapids. I just sat in my seat and held on for the ride.

We arrived in Grand Rapids about an hour later than he wanted and pulled into the Grand Am Hotel. We had a nice room on the second floor just above the area where people pull into the hotel and drop off their luggage. Before I knew what was happening Claude was on the phone. He cleaned up a bit and he was off. I thought what was going on. I was looking out the window of our room and I saw his appointment. The lady drove up and he jumped in. I knew I was on my own from that minute. It was dinner time so I went to their restaurant in the hotel because Claude did not leave me the keys to his car. Claude knew the area well because he went to school there but it was a new area for me. I walked around for over an hour after dinner and went back to the room for the night. I thought Claude was coming back but I was wrong. I woke up at 6:00 a.m. and Claude's bed was not disturbed. I decided to get ready for the day on meetings scheduled throughout the hotel when I looked outside. The same lady drove up and dropped Claude off at around 7:00 a.m. They had been together all night. I thought maybe they just talked all night. Boy was I wrong. Claude could hardly get himself out of her car. He tripped on the sidewalk but picked himself up in a short amount of time. He came into our room a few minutes later in what I would call bad shape. I knew what I was looking at because my father was an alcoholic woman chaser and Claude looked about the same. I left our room and went to the conference meetings in Claude's place. Now it all made sense. His appointment with this brown haired woman, the speeding and his statement about what happens in Grand Rapids stays in Grand Rapids. I knew at this point I could never trust him again. Anyone who cheats on his or her spouse will cheat on anything. Claude woke up after I arrived back into our room after the conference sessions were over for the day. I took notes, met a lot of people and went out with Claude and some other superintendents for dinner. Claude was so tired he decided to go back to our room for the night. He had gotten what he wanted out of this trip and we drove home the next morning. This time his speed was legal and we made it home safe and sound. I also decided if we go anywhere again I would do the driving. He never mentioned the conference on the trip home. We said little to each other on the way to Standish. I felt sorry for Claude's wife, Christine, but now knew what I was in for. I knew to much and the rest of my time at Standish-Sterling would be working for a man I could not trust. How can a person trust someone who cheats on the one he is suppose to love?

Chapter VII

TIME AFTER TIME/ FOOT BY FOOT

ROUND NUMBER ONE

The conference trip now opened my eyes for the first time at Standish-Sterling. Claude was the type of educational leader who tried to paint a picture of a very intelligent man. The one thing that drove him nuts was if someone would call him stupid or say that was a stupid thing to do. I believe it all had something to do with his relationship with his father. He actually hated his father and had nothing to do with him what-so-ever. His parents divorced years before and he must have blamed his father. Just maybe his father knew him better than anyone. I did not know Claude before I came to Standish but I could never break the bond people put on us as one and the same. This was as far from the truth as one could get. Since the conference in Grand Rapids nothing he would ever do could surprise me. He was actually afraid of his own shadow. If someone had a cold Claude would stay far away thinking he would certainly catch it. He was exactly the opposite of what most people thought. He would say he acted for the benefit of the students but I knew he was out for himself and nothing more. I was not surprised when he told me he never bought his daughter a Christmas gift. One year he bought her a Hi-Fi System but decided to take it back and give it to himself. Something was strange about this man. The School Board hired him just before he hired me. James Polls, a Claude supporter, told me he was the only Board member who wanted him after the interviews for a superintendent at the time. He said he convinced the remaining Board members to hire Claude and he regretted it ever since.

For a number of years the Board tried to get rid of him and always found out his contract Claude wrote was to binding. The Board would have to pay him at least three years salary plus many other concessions. The Board and Mr. Foot never worked well together but the Board had no choice. I know of two other times the Board tried to break his contract without buying him out. Knowing what they thought of Claude I could only imagine what they thought of me. Claude always told his administrators we would go before him because he had a binding three-year contract and we only had a non-binding two-year administrative one. He liked to hold that over our heads year after year. I knew how the other administrators felt about Claude and like it or not I was his only supporter out of this group.

One day Mr. Critz called me on the phone to set up a meeting with all the administrators except Mr. Foot. It was scheduled for my office on a day we could all make it. This meeting included the principals of the two elementary schools, the junior high principal, the curriculum director and myself. I found out they wanted a piece of the pie Claude was eating from. Claude treated his administrators like shit to say the least. He would bargain with his favorite group the teachers while he treated the non-certified pretty bad and his administrators the worse. It was like we were scum and owed everything we had to him. That was what he called loyalty. Boy, was he wrong. Loyalty is like most things. It works both ways. How could he expect loyalty from us when we were treated the way we were. Claude would never listen to us because he thought we were low life but still expected us to be loyal to him in whatever he was doing. He totally missed the boat in my opinion. The group wanted a little of what Mr. Foot had in his contract. Not one of them had the nerve to approach him but chose me to talk with him for the group. They thought I was his only friend and could do the job. I finally said ok and went to talk to Mr. Foot the next day. I had written and typed everything the group wanted and scheduled a meeting with him after school. I walked into his office and handed Mr. Foot a copy of what we wanted. I was shocked at what his next move was. He threw the paper in his wastebasket saying he already knew what was inside and his answer was no. He would not even discuss anything with me. I found out a day later that Mr. Roger Sanderson, the curriculum director, told Claude everything the group discussed. Now, I knew we had a traitor in the group and we were dead in the water.

My relationship with Mr. Foot changed from that day on. He was always putting the blame on my shoulders even if I had nothing to do with something to begin with. He was not the type of person who could take the blame on anything someone did not like. He was a weak individual who I believe was ready for a nervous breakdown. He knew where he stood in the community and like most people wanted to switch the blame to someone other than himself. I was the one he chose from that day on. I was aware of what he was doing and believed in always doing the right thing. It was my own fault for believing in others but I did. I once told him I would never lie to or for him or anyone else. I had to be myself and be proud of what I saw in the mirror. I do have a fault and that's swearing. It relieves my frustrations and I see nothing wrong with it as long as it does not get out of hand.

The echo was running wild. They were coming about as fast as they could for a few years right after the superintendent's conference in Grand Rapids. Claude never knew what I saw at the conference and I was not about to bring it up.

DENNY II

Things were coming together for the next few years at Standish-Sterling Central High School. I was lucky to have Mr. Dennis Smith as my assistant principal for around thirteen years. We worked well together and we were extremely loyal to each other. Denny was called Denny II by the staff and I was Denny I. Denny II was from the staff and had been a math teacher until I arrived. We hit it off from the very beginning. We trusted each other and he knew the staff much better than I because he was one of them. We shared information with each other about each member of the staff as well as Mr. Foot. He and I will always be great friends. He wanted to be a principal and at the time I was not planning on looking for another job. Denny II started looking for greener pastures getting recommendations from people he worked with and/or knew quite well. Claude and I were included until Denny II decided it was hurting his chances in getting a job if he used Claude on his resume. It seemed the other superintendents knew Claude and did not care much for him. They felt sorry for me too having to he his second in command and they asked me many times how I could stand it. I told them it was hard but I always thought I could work with anyone as long as I respected them and/ or what they were doing. I still believe it even though I had my doubts about Mr. Foot. Getting back to Denny II he finally applied at Sanford-Meridian for a principal position and did what I recommended to him. I told him not to use Mr. Foot as a recommendation and see how things would go. The superintendent called me on Denny II and Sanford-Meridian Schools hired him the next day. It worked for Denny II like I thought it would even though I never wanted to see him go. I wished him the best and we parted as great friends as we are today.

JOB HUNTING

I started to apply for other jobs right after Denny II left. It was not something I wanted to ever do again in my life but Claude was getting harder to work with each and every year. One year I was interviewed for the principal position at Bangor High School in Bay City, Michigan. The interview went well and I knew they were going to offer me the position. I had done my student teaching experience at their middle school and my supervising teacher, Mrs. Stanley, thought very highly of me and my abilities as a teacher. She was the one who years before got me my first teaching job at St. Stephen's Area High School in Saginaw. She told me when she retired she wanted me to take her place at Bangor because I was her best student teacher she had ever had. But when the time came the superintendent had a friend who had a wife with the same degree and because of that alone he chose her. This was the first time I finally realized it was not what a person knows or even how good a person is it's who you know that matters. This is how most jobs are filled and that's that. Before Bangor called me about that principal position I chose to have a talk with Mr. Foot. He did not want me to go at the time and told me he would try to change. I believed him and I felt my job was not over at Standish-Sterling so I called and wrote a letter to the superintendent at Bangor and told him I was going to stay at Standish-Sterling before he offered me the position. A year before I left Standish-Sterling a friend at Tawas Area High School was retiring as high school principal and the superintendent wanting me to come to Tawas. I never knew what was about to happen at Standish-Sterling and I told them thanks for offering me their position but I was not interested because I did not want to go further North than I was. The Lord works in mysterious ways sometimes.

TWENTY-FOUR SEVEN

The next thing I knew was Claude called me over to his office. He had received a call from a mother who had some information she wanted it to be checked out. He said the four students had been drinking in the woods and ran into a tree. He wanted me to find out and let him know. I always did what he wanted because he was my boss even though I had no interest in the matter. Standish-Sterling had a school board policy I did not believe in and never heard of before in my life. The policy for athletes is a lifetime commitment made by the students once they go out for a sport or participate on a team representing Standish-Sterling. The student may go out for cheerleading or a sport in the seventh grade and once that is done they fall under the policy until they graduate. They are punished for the first offense for drinking, smoking and gross misbehavior of any type. They must attend a class before they can participate ever again. They are off the squad and/or team if they are caught again and cannot go out from that day on until they graduate.

The policy was presented to the board by the coaches long before I arrived at the school and the board was not willing to consider anything else. If these students were seen by anyone at any time and let's say were drinking wine with their parents at a formal event the policy went into effect. This could be for six years of the student's life. Each case had to be checked out on its' own merits and it actually made students and parents lie about any type incident going against the policy. It made sense from a coach's point of view but did it resolve the problems? Did these students stop drinking? If a student was seen let's say at a local wedding by a coach he or she just broke the policy and to my knowledge it was enforced. I remember Mr. Foot telling the junior high principal if his son ever broke the policy it would be enforced. That was fine with the junior high principal as long as it was being enforced on everyone and it was not. Mr. Foot had a daughter and with her friend got into his wine one evening according to Claude himself but he did not want her punished. It seems as though this policy was good for everyone else but not his own.

In getting back to the four students, I decided to talk to each one individually and see what information I would get. I chose the local sheriff's youngest daughter and she told me everything I wanted to know. She was and still is as honest as the day is long. The other three students denied their involvement and I went to Claude with what I found out. I told him I believed the sheriff's daughter and everyone was drinking. Just before this happened the local sheriff, James Mullski told the school's administrators he was going to give us a copy of whatever passed his desk about this type of thing happening with our students throughout the state. He had the information each week across his desk. Needless to say with his daughter being part of this case no information was ever shared with the school.

The fact of the matter was the sheriff went to the board and wanted me fired for talking to the students without him being there. I told him I used the same method he uses in his office. It's called divide and conquer and it usually works. The local sheriff seemed to be satisfied with the policy but he did not want it enforced on his daughter. Actually, only one of the boys, ever participated in a sport during his high school career. It did not matter for the other three in this incident. The boy was a senior who never planned to play again and was graduating in June. I was always against this policy because it was not being enforced on everyone. This fact made it wrong from the start. The board took action and supported me on this one but the wheels were in motion.

I thought this was a good time for the sheriff to support his daughter for telling the truth about the incident but that did not happen. Like I said before he was taking the matter to the board. Before listening to what he had to say I found out he went to see Mr. Foot. The sheriff wanted to know who called him with the information and Claude denied knowing anything about it. I did not know what was happening so I went to his office and asked him why he lied to the sheriff. He told me someone had to keep communications open between the school and the sheriff's office. I told him thanks a lot for lying and making me look bad. That's what I get for trusting him again while he set me up instead of telling the sheriff the truth ending the matter. Claude actually wanted me to go along with him and I him I could never do what he wanted and live and respect myself. Claude took it as being disloyal to him and really didn't care about me at all. The problem was this would lead to a small group of people in the Standish-Sterling Community hating me from this day on. I had to keep quiet and not discuss the incident with anyone. The sheriff and his wife wanted me gone for doing my job. It could have worked out for them and their daughter for standing up and telling the truth. In my opinion the parents pressure did more harm than they could imagine. What they had taught her was now and forever destroyed. I lost my respect for the local sheriff and his wife along with my boss again. I knew what he was doing but no one really cares unless they are directly involved. It's a sad thing to say but that's the type of society we now live in. Think about what's happening in our nation and the entire world. I would bet everything I have the truth will never come out on most matters. These two individuals will play a significant role in my forced retirement later. I think the sheriff and I actually became friends after all was said and done.

FFA

In the summer of the same year Claude again called me over. I was getting a little gun shy of his approach and the echo was again running its course. He asked me if I knew what Bob Tein was making during the summer months. Bob would take his teaching salary during the academic year and rely on running the FFA activities in the summer. He had been doing this for a number of years. Claude took a look at what he was paid and went nuts. He asked me to have Bob make out a sheet stating the time he spent doing his summer job and let him know. At this point I did not know what they were paying Bob and really did not care. I met with Bob the next day and asked him to keep a log on his time he worked on FFA activities for the next few weeks. Two weeks later he gave me a copy and I brought it to Claude.

Claude looked over the information Bob had given me and said the amount Bob gets per hour is more than he makes and it will have to be changed. Claude said it was over $50.00 an hour and was way too much for what he was doing. I never knew what they were paying Bob and really didn't care.

Bob will never go down as a great teacher but he was worth his weight in gold with the farmers and within the entire community. That's a lot of gold if you know Bob. He was also a father figure to many students who never had an adult figure they could trust and believe in. The problem was Bob told the farmers I was messing with him by checking on his hours and his rate of pay. The president of the FFA alumni finally went to see Mr. Foot about what was going on with Bob. Claude again acted like he did not know what was actually taking place. He did tell the president of the FFA Alumni he would work things out with Bob and he did. The agreement was what I suggested to Mr. Foot. The agreement lowered Bob's pay to what the people in our community education department received by the hour. Again I looked like the bad guy because Mr. Foot ordered me to look into the matter. I guess it was part of my job but the plank kept getting a little shorter every time I took a walk over to Claude's office.

GUN

The next thing I knew I received a call at home from Mr. Foot. He told me the janitors were busy cleaning the classrooms and they found a gun in one. It was in a box wide open to the students. It was not loaded but in the box was two full clips of shells. I told him I would be right over. When I arrived at the school a janitor told me whose room the gun was found in and who was already in the room. I walked in with the janitor and saw Mr. Foot, another janitor and the local sheriff. The teacher was not notified yet and she was not present. The gun was still in the wide-open box on the bookshelf under the class windows. I told everyone I would go back to my office and call the teacher at home. She was home and acted totally unaware of any gun in her room. I asked her to come right over and she said she would be right there. She lived over thirty miles away and the wait seemed like forever. We all waited as she arrived around 45 minutes later. The local sheriff asked her if she knew the gun was in the room and she said she had no idea and could not believe it had been found in her classroom. She acted like she was in total shock. I thought she was going to get sick over the situation for a while and she asked if she could leave and go home. The sheriff took the gun back to his office and everyone went home. I thought it was all a bunch of crap and knew something was not on the up-and-up. About an hour after I was home the teacher called me. She said she was looking for her husband and finally found him. I knew what she was going to say before a word was uttered. She said she knew the gun was in her classroom with two full clips. I said she was putting the security of her students in harms way. She said there was nothing she could do about it because it was her husband's gun and she could not make him take it back home. I asked her why she didn't tell me about the gun. At least I would have taken it out of her classroom. I asked her why she lied to us at school? She said she wanted to talk to her husband first but could not find him when I called her. He husband was an aid for one of our blind students and had done a great job with him. I asked her why her husband brought the gun to school in the first place? She said one of our seniors was carrying on and her husband thought if anything bad was going to happen he was going to protect the students, his wife and himself.

The sad thing was the senior was no danger to anyone. He had been expelled but drove through the parking lot once to my knowledge. I told him to leave and I never saw him again around school. I did see him later and found out he finished high school and received his diploma. He gave me a big hug and we parted.

I reported the call I received to Mr. Foot right after the teacher called me. He said he would think about it and get back to me. He asked me what I thought should be done? I told him she was not one of my strongest teachers on staff and she was finishing up her 25th. year at Standish-Sterling. I told him he should listen to both the teacher and her husband as quickly as possible and make a decision soon. Claude was never a man to let someone know what he was thinking and the hotter the issue the longer his decision would take. I once asked our head of maintenance why he left his position and he said it took Foot to long to give him an answer on anything even if it had to be taken care of right away. He said after a while it pissed him off and that was that. But that's another short story. I waited for Mr. Foot to let me know what he was going to do because other teachers, students and parents wanted to know. In a small community word spreads faster than the wind can blow. I went over to his office and told Mr. Foot what I would do the very next day. I told him I would get rid of her as soon as possible. She knew about the gun, lied to us and never let us know the gun was in the building. The intent of the gun being in the building according to the teacher and her husband was to harm the senior if need be. I told Mr. Foot the teacher was finishing her 25-year and even if the school district had to pay she might be bought off but she had to go. That was my position and I would and could not change my mind.

Any student who either brought a knife and/or gun to school was expelled. How could one do any different for a teacher? But, Mr. Foot was not feeling good about the whole situation. He was still thinking about what to do at this point. Like always he wanted to look good in the community and I could tell he wanted someone else to handle it while he did absolutely nothing.

It was finally settled by Claude giving it to a retired teacher who was the teacher's best friend who taught across the hall from her for those twenty-five years. This person was now on the school board for only one purpose and one purpose only. She wanted to get Mr. Foot and myself no matter what. Mrs. Joan Harmond was her name. Needless to say nothing was ever done to the teacher and her husband took the blame and he resigned from the school. Mr. Foot had what he wanted and he did not have to get involved. In my opinion he stayed a true coward once again. As for Joan, she and I would go at it on a few more occasions in the future.

CARDS

The junior high principal hired a new teacher from Midland, Michigan who was doing a good job. The junior high was in the same building as the high school at the time. Her classroom was out in a portable trailer unit in the back of the building. She came to me one day with a complaint about her principal and wanted to know why he was doing nothing about her cards. I never heard about her cards but they were missing for around two months when she came to me. I contacted the head of maintenance and we walked around the building trying to figure things out. It looked as though someone had to have a key to get into the room. It was a large collection of cards so we assumed no student could have done it. I then asked Matt LaDeau (the head of maintenance) what janitor was working the night the cards disappeared. Matt said he had a sub for the regular janitor on the evening in question.

I said he had to be the one. I told Matt to call him to get the cards back or we were going to the authorities. Matt came back to my office in about ten minutes and told me he admitted to taking the cards. He was going to bring them back within a few minutes and he did. I brought them to the teacher and told her what happened. She was happy to get her cards back and we both thought this was the end. Boy, were we wrong. I did not know she went to the association before coming to me. The president of the association was you guessed it, Joan Harmond. I did not give it a second thought but the teacher came to see me once again. She explained to me Joan had written a letter to the school board saying the administration had done nothing to help this teacher find her cards. Because, I was running both the senior and junior high school programs, Joan was once again trying to get me. The first thing I did was to ask Joan to a meeting. The teacher again explained the situation to Joan telling her I found the cards the same day I became aware of the situation. The teacher could not believe Joan would not budge on her letter because she had a different agenda. I saw her letter and it was full of lies just trying to make me look bad. Joan sent the letter anyways. A few days later the teacher was so mad at what Joan did she told me she was going to send the board a letter telling them what actually happened. She sent her letter to the board members but it really didn't matter at this point. The board thought I told her to send her letter but I had nothing to do with it. The teacher was so upset she decided to resign after spending only one year with us because of what Joan had done to her and myself.

I believe this points out what and whom I was working with during my time at

Standish-Sterling Central High School. I could not trust anyone at this point and I watched my ass from that day on.

FRENCH TRIP

I hired a new French teacher right out of college who seemed to be doing a good job with her classes except for one student. He was a senior and he and her did not get along at all. The senior was extremely intelligent and knew what buttons to push to get her to lose control in her classroom. It did not seem like a day went by she did not send him to my office. I finally said enough was enough and I decided to put him on independent study for the remainder of the year. It seemed to work for both of them. The teacher could now settle down and do her job. The senior was not being sent to my office every time I turned around. But they both still hated each other. All this senior had to do was look at her and things would happen again.

The senior was ranked number two in his class and was going to be the class salutatorian at graduation. He was a true leader in his class and served as Student Council President for his junior and senior years. He and I worked together very well on every school project that came up for those two years. I never had to worry about him doing his job because he usually had it done way before hand. He seemed to be in complete control and knew what he wanted out of his life. I was so impressed with him I knew he would accomplish his goals in life. There were not too many students I could say this about over my 34 years in education. He and I were best of friends and we both knew what the other was thinking before anything was ever said.

One day I heard the French teacher and another tenured teacher wanted to take her advanced French class to France for a school trip. I think you know how I would feel about another trip so I told them to see how much support they would have from the students and their parents and I would recommend it to the school board. The parents and school board were all in favor of the trip and I recommended it at the monthly board meeting. I would have never agreed to the trip if she was going by herself. But that was not the case. The trip was planned to the finest detail and everyone was ready to depart.

The day before the trip I had a one-on-one talk with the senior she could never get along with. After the meeting I decided to call the senior's mother at work and ask her not to send her son. I did not know if something was going to happen and I did not want to take the chance. The mother worked at the local hospital and I got her right away. I told her not to send her son on the trip but she would not listen. She said he worked very hard during his years in high school and deserved going on the trip. She said he earned it and he was going. I again asked her not to send him but her mind was made up.

Sometimes I get those feelings about something is going to happen for the negative. The echo was chiming once again. To me it's like three knocks on the door without anyone being there. Something was going to happen and I did not want to know what it was going to be.

I believe the two teachers and the students were only in France a short time when things started to happen. The senior student whose mother I had talked to was acting up and it was getting to the teachers. I did not know this until the trip was over but I wish the teacher had called me from France. I could have at least talked to him once again.

I finally received a call from the French teacher telling me the senior boy had been caught drinking a beer in a café. I asked her if she was going to send him home and she said no. After the call I never heard a word until the group arrived back in Standish. I met with the two teachers ASAP. They told me the senior was a big pain for them the entire trip but they got through it and made it back safely. Because the trip was board sponsored the rules of the school now had to be enforced. The senior knew what was coming and what it meant for him. The teachers wanted him disciplined by the school for drinking alcohol. I would not expect anything else at that point. I was in full support of the teachers until I investigated the trip a little more by talking with the other students.

The students totally enjoyed taking the trip to France but other things happened making the senior no guiltier than the teachers and other students. I found out during the trip the teachers took the group through a wine factory. This was not on their agenda for the trip and I wondered why. The teachers never gave me a reason when I asked them. They both thought it would be educational for the students. During the tour through the wine factory the students decided to buy bottles of wine if the teachers would bring it through customs in New York. The teachers told the students they would and it was smuggled through. The students did not drink the wine but were in possession of it after they left New York and returned back to Standish. I wondered who was guiltier at this point? The senior who was caught drinking a beer or the other students for buying it. How about the two teachers who smuggled it back for the students?

By the time I told the Superintendent, Mr. Claude L. Foot, what I found out he already knew. His secretary or administrative assistant as she was called had a son on the trip along with a board member's daughter. He told Denny II and I he wanted the senior boy given at least three days off and nothing would happen to the other students while the two teachers would be docked with two days off. Mr. Smith and I went back to my office and we could not believe what we were hearing from our boss. Again, who was guilty and/or guiltier?

Denny II and I had both agreed the senior boy should not be punished any more than the others. In fact, a person only has to be seventeen to legally drink in France. The senior boy was beyond seventeen. That was our recommendation to Claude. Claude then called us over to his office once again. I told him I would never sign the letter suspending the senior from school and not the others. It was a clear case of who you were instead of doing what was right and I refused to be part of it. I thought I would be fired for my refusal but I have to live with myself and keep my self-respect. Without that I was nothing and nobody could ever take it away. In Claude's eyes I was being disloyal to him but I saw it another way altogether. Claude finally talked Denny II into suspending the senior for three days and he thought it was over.

The story did not end there. The senior just before the French trip had received a letter confirming his appointment to West Point Academy. I had written a letter for him and we were both happy he got in. His parents were very proud of their son's achievements and thought they knew this was what he wanted. How much better could it get?

The senior didn't seem to upset being suspended from school for three days. He told us he called West Point and told them what happened. He was a proud and honest student who always stood up for what he believed. I truly believe going to West Point was his mother's dream and not his. That was why he called them and they took his commission away for having a beer in France and given three days off. The estimated cost of this commission was around $500,000.00 at the time. It would have been a great education to receive but things didn't work out. I would have never called West Point at the time. I believe he deserved the time off but how about the other students and teachers who bought wine and smuggled it back to the United States.

The other students received nothing while the French teacher received three days off without pay. The tenured teacher won her case in arbitration and received nothing for her actions either. But, the incident was not over yet and the echoes were coming fast and strong.

On Thursday of that week and the last day of our senior's suspension, I had just returned from West Branch. The special event was a luncheon for all the top academic students in our conference. Each school brought their top ten senior students with a combination of academic GPA and ACT scores. They were put on either first, second or third team and each received a medallion and certificate. Each school paid for their luncheon and the students had the rest of the afternoon off. It was nice time for all and students get to meet each other as academic leaders and not competing against each other in an athletic contest.

When the luncheon was over I would always take them to the local dairy in West Branch for a little treat.

When I returned, I parked in front of the administration building of the district. I went into Mr. Foot's office to let him know how things went at the luncheon. I was giving my report when all hell broke loose. The district bookkeeper came screaming into Mr. Foot's office. She said our senior was outside in the parking lot and he had a gun. Denny II and I ran out of Mr. Foot's office as fast as we could to see what was happening. I could not believe my eyes. The senior had a loaded rifle (AK 47 with armor piercing bullets) and he was headed for the school building. Denny II and a janitor tackled him as fast as they could. While they were holding him down I grabbed the gun and his keys for the van he was driving. I unloaded the rifle noticing a few more boxes of shells and locked his van with the rifle and shells in it and went out to see how I could help. I yelled to the bookkeeper to call 911 and have the building locked down.

The senior's older brother was also there. I remember how hard it was for him to watch what was going on. This was one of the saddest moments of both of our lives. I had always bragged about the senior but didn't know about his temper. The local under sheriff came and took the senior away. Before taking him away I asked him who was he going to shoot with the gun? He said he was going to walk into the school and just start shooting at anyone moving. I could see for the time he had lost it. He was out of control.

Denny II and I walked back into Mr. Foot's office because we did not see him outside. He was hiding behind a file cabinet when we saw him. He said he wasn't going to get shot by that crazy bastard and moved from behind the file. Both Denny II and I were not surprised by his actions. We knew he was a coward from the start. He hated anything confrontational and always blamed someone else for his screw-ups. Can you imagine how many times I was blamed for things Mr. Foot had done over my years at Standish-Sterling. It became quite sickening time after time.

The senior was expelled from school and carried stipulations on him for many years to come. His salutatorian award was still given to him along with his high school diploma after the graduation ceremonies were over. I wonder sometimes if this would have been a teacher, what would have been the punishment? Because Mr. Foot had given in and was only protecting himself I would bet a teacher would have gotten off without a day's suspension like in the past.

FINAL EXAM

Final exams were taking place at the end of the first semester and I was walking the halls to make sure the students stayed in their rooms and not out roaming the halls disturbing other students. Everything was running like clockwork until I spotted a girl getting something out of her locker. We had known each other for four years at the time. She was an outstanding student and athlete who I really respected at the time. I could only guess what was about to happen next. She shut her locker as fast as she could when she spotted me standing in the hall. I walked over to her and asked to see what she was reading and she threw it back in her locker. She did not want to open her locker and I knew something was wrong. I told her I had a key and if I had to, I would open it myself. She finally decided to open it. The piece of paper she did not want me to see was a copy of her final exam she was going to take next hour. She did not know what to say next so

I walked her across the hall into her English teacher's classroom. The girl stayed out in the hallway while the teacher and I talked about the exam the girl had. The teacher was the same one who had the gun in her classroom later. The teacher told me it was her exam she was going to give next hour. She wondered how this young girl had a copy of it. The girl would not tell us, so I walked her to my office and we talked. My daughter (Terri) was in her class and had many classes with her in school. I kept my door open, as I have always done with female students in my office. She finally told me the truth after we spent time together talking about many different issues of no particular interest and/or the exam. She was a great girl and seemed to tell me the truth all the time.

I knew the students were cheating constantly in their classes for better grades. The rumors were all around the school. I had just had a staff meeting and told the teachers what was going on and we had to put a stop to it. So, I was on lookout. Sure enough the rumor came true and it almost cost me my job. The girl finally told me her and three of her friends had purchased the exam from another student for $2.00. The four studied it at my neighbor's house the night before. I checked with the other three students and they all admitted it and their involvement. I decided to give each student an F on their final exam and suspended them from school for cheating. In a way this teacher made it to easy for the students to cheat in her class. All year long students had been going up to her desk for questions about the test they were having. She had the answer sheet on her desk. Each student would memorize let's say five answers. The next student would take the next five and so on until the students had them all if they didn't have the test before taking it. Students are smart and seem to outdo any teacher in this school. They will cheat if the teacher gives them a chance. This teacher was so bad I do not believe she knew what day it was without someone telling her. The students knew it. Another problem was she received tenure long before I came and had job security for life no matter what. I could only talk to her and write her up but that fell on deaf ears.

I once had two teachers who were actually in heat. The one was recently divorced and the male thought he was superman. He would always say he was trying to help by counseling them.

I say them because there was many more than one. As I would go into either one of their classrooms they would wait till I left and then meet in the other's classroom. This went on for quite some time. I finally waited in the halls and caught them red handed. I wrote them up and took it to Mr. Foot, the superintendent. He ended up tossing it in the waste bucket saying it was worthless. It would be their word against mine. Because the district was and still is being run by the teachers he figured he knew how it was going to end. The teachers and their friends and families can control any election for the board and this was again just proven in the district's last board election. Claude was not willing to go against a teacher for anything. He was gone if he pissed off a certain family and/or teacher who was known around the district. Remember, he only cared about himself and nobody else. So, I quit writing the teachers up unless it was for something damaging to a student. I just had to look the other way when something like this happened. It happened time after time.

The incident seemed to be over until the young lady had to tell her parents. Her father was a teacher in the district and knew what buttons to pull. His daughter seemed to forget everything she had told me. Before I knew it the whole event was going to the board once again. The girl's father had made a call to the other student's parents for help in winning this issue. He wanted my ass out only because it was his daughter who was caught and not someone else. I would have had his full support if it would have been another student but it was not. His problem was the other three boys were very close to me as principal/student relationship goes. One student lives just down the road and his parents and I are very close friends. His mother told me she had seen the four students studying something the night before the exam at her house but she did not know what it was. Now they knew. They knew their son was guilty and they would not help the girl's father by lying to the board. Another parent of another boy was my bowling and golf partner and great friend and he told the parent to go to hell. As it worked out all three boys admitted to what they had done and his protest against my actions were thrown out by the board. Mr. Foot like always stayed the same. He sat and said nothing in my support.

The sad thing was the girl student never told me she was sorry. She wanted to get into the school's National Honor Society for her last two years of high school I would not let her in until she talked to me again. She never did and I refused letting her in to the NHS until Mr. Foot forced me to put her in against my wishes. He threatened me over my job if I would not let her in. I figured what the hell there are many jobs out there and my self-respect was still in tact. I signed her card and she became a member of the NHS her senior year. By the way she has never talked to me again.

Like the sheriff this parent taught his child a lesson she will never forget. When it comes down to your children lying is ok. Sometimes I wonder about this generation becoming habitual liars because I see it all the time. Another math teacher at Standish-Sterling would read a book while many of his students cheated on their tests and final exams. When I approached him about what he was doing he said theirs would come later in life. He never changed his testing ways and retired a few years later.

The person I felt the sorriest for during this time was my daughter, Terri. Terri went to a school her father was principal of. She had to work hard for her grades while her older brother Gary found school easy. Gary graduated from Bay City Handy six years before and ended up in the top honor group of his class. Terri knew what was going on in her classes but could not do anything about it. We talked many times about what the other students were doing while teachers didn't seem to care. I don't believe she ever cheated like the rest and worked her butt off for the grades she earned. I believe in the end it has helped her become a better person and mother. I could not be more proud of what she has accomplished so far in life. But I would never again send her to a school I was principal of. She could hardly ever be a normal child by doing something wrong. I know other students would put pressure on her to do what they were doing. For the most part she refused and I'm glad she did. She ended up graduating in the highest honor group in her class. She is now a RN in Saginaw while her brother is a CPA in Chicago. Dad could not be happier and extremely proud of what they both became in life. Hopefully they will make a positive contribution to our society. At least Gloria and I taught them something positive they will remember us far after our time comes. As for myself I no longer worry about them being a good person and/or taking care of them. They will do just fine in this sometimes crazy and mixed up world we live in. Our lessons have been noted and received.

TEACHER-STUDENT AFFAIRS

When I first came to Standish-Sterling Community Schools I was told about many teacher-student affairs going on for years with nothing happening even though everyone seemed to know about at least a few. I could not believe my ears and would have to wait and see for myself. This was something that only happens in screwed up districts and I thought better of Standish-Sterling. Well was I wrong. As time unfolded I discovered and actually seen for myself. If it was only a few over the course of time and before I got there I might not have cared so much. It was like a plague and people sort of let these affairs go on and looked the other way. When I hear about these affaires on television I am no longer surprised. I am surprised at the outcome in many school districts.

When I was in high school in the Bay City System I knew about one teacher who did this all the time. He was finally caught having sex with a student and was fired from his teaching position. He fought it for many years until the girl wanted to get on with her life and leave the area. He had his union behind him and together they finally won in court. I wondered what a bunch of B.S. I had this same teacher in school and knew the girls he had affairs with and the ones who would clean his house for an A in his classroom. One girl in my class knew absolutely nothing about the subject he taught but received an A for her final grade. I know this was not for what she knew but for what she gave him. He was one low life and should have been taken out altogether. Like I said this teacher's case went on for years. The girl finally wanted to move on with her life and didn't want to be involved anymore. I could not blame her.

In the end the teacher was reinstated as a teacher and was moved to another high school in the district and taught at a lower level. He received his back pay for a number of years with credit for those years he was off along with his pension. This case is public knowledge in Bay City and now I was facing a similar situation in Standish-Sterling. At this point I could name at least eight teachers who have had sex with female students under their care. Four are now retired while at least four are still teaching in the school district. I witnessed letters coming through the school's mail for these teachers coming from the students themselves. Another teacher finally married the girl and later retired from teaching.

One night after a scheduled parent-teacher conference I was making my rounds around the school locking things up for the night. I opened a teacher's door and a teacher said for me not to come in his classroom or turn on the lights. I knew what was going on because I could still see what was happening with the hallway lights still being turned on. I backed out of the doorway and went to find anyone else. I thought I could find a janitor but they were done for the night and had left. I quickly thought of what I could do next. Nobody else was around except the teacher, the female student and myself. So I moved my vehicle out of sight and waited until the two left the building. I was in shock when I saw who the girl was in the light. I knew her and her family for years. The teacher was the same one I caught moving around to another teacher's room after I had left. He was no surprise because I knew what he was like for a long time. But now he was with a student. I knew I had to do something. This was my legal obligation. I called Mr. Foot as soon as I got home. He was tired and said he would see me first thing the next morning. I was not surprised. I could just see where this was going. When I met with my boss, Mr. Foot, his response was exactly what I thought it would be. He said it would end up being their word against mine and the teacher would win. I said who cares and wanted this man out of not only my building but also not being around children altogether. But Mr. Foot said no way and that was the end. I could write the same teacher up again but Mr. Foot would do the same thing he had done before. I was really pissed but I again had no support. I could have contacted the sheriff but that would have made no difference. So seeing it with my own eyes meant nothing and the issue never surfaced again.

Chapter VIII

DUAL ENROLLMENT

ROUND NUMBER TWO

The governor of the state of Michigan sent out a letter to all the high school principals and superintendents. The letter was covering the criteria going to be used for high school students who qualified for dual enrollment. This meant high school students could go to their high school and college at the same time with the students home district paying for the student's college classes if they qualified. I ran a copy of the letter and was ready to send it to the parents when Mr. Foot stopped me.

He told me not to send the letter the way it was. He wanted to make some changes and then I could send it after I signed it. Boy, this was no great surprise. So I waited to see what was going to happen next. He actually retyped the letter changing the qualifications students would have to meet before they could participate in this educational program. Mr. Foot told me he did not want his money to go to any college in the area. This was the first time I had heard him call it his money and not the districts. He would always refer to the money as his from that day on. As tight as he was he thought it belonged to him. For the past ten years school budgets never increased while everything was getting more expensive. In fact for a few years after budgets were not given out to the buildings. If a building needed money to spend only Mr. Foot could authorize the purchase. I remember the math department head wanted to buy new books for a general course. Mr. Foot told Denny II and I to tell him no six different times. Finally the department head went to see Mr. Foot himself. Before we knew what was happening Mr. Foot ok'd his request and authorized the purchase of the textbooks. Denny II and I were so upset we went to see. Mr. Foot. He said he was the boss and he could do whatever he wanted to if he chose to do so. He then asked us to leave because he was working on his portfolio. Surprise! Surprise!

The state's letter to the parents stated if their son and/or daughter passed just the math portion of the MEAP test given by the state students could take a math course in college while going to high school with the school district flipping the bill. This could save the parents a lot of money while giving the students college credits. I thought it was a great idea and had the University of Michigan offer a Government course to our students over the Internet. Our students did well with all of them receiving an A in the course. This meant the students now had three credits at the U.of M. It was paid for by the district. As for the students who wanted to take a course at a two-year college Mr. Foot changed the letter to the parents stating the students had to pass all their MEAP's before they were allowed to dual enroll. Mr. Foot's letter went against the state law and many of our students were not able to participate in this wonderful program. When he finished changing the letter he brought it over to me to sign but I chose not to put my signature on it. Instead someone in the office used a stamp with my signature on it and then sent them out to the parents. I did have a counselor who was an eyewitness to what had taken place for my own protection. I was learning to cover my ass once again. I had been using my tape recorder from the first superintendence's conference. I would finish my career at Standish-Sterling with 27 tapes of what actually took place and not what Mr. Foot was telling everyone and blaming everything on me. Maybe someday I'll get to use them in a court of law. By the time all this was taking place I was also using my digital camera and have a lot of pictures to go along with my tapes. The way I looked at it was I was only protecting myself because as Mr. Foot would say time after time to all the administrators to cover your ass because nobody cares. So I covered my ass whenever I could. His statement was made year after year around the time the school board did his evaluation. He would get so depressed he would always tell us to look for another job because it was no picnic for him. At this point I was seriously thinking about moving and could not stand or trust him anymore pertaining to any matter that came up.

He was running scared and now the school board was calling the shots. I was still somewhat loyal to Mr. Foot and kept him informed on what was happening until the day he ordered me to go down to one of the elementary buildings. I actually stopped looking for another job when my daughter got married and became pregnant for the first time. I wanted to live around my grandchild and did not want to move. This was when I was offered two other positions and turned them down. My family has always been my number one priority. A person can always find another job but a family is a full time commitment for life. Her husband was and is a great guy, and father who still works as a janitor in the middle school at Standish-Sterling.

When I think about the money the district saved by not allowing most of their students the chance to dual enroll it makes me sick. If you did not notice Claude's name was never attached to the letter he changed from the state but you can bet your life that he did. He was the only one he was concerned about and hardly ever the students. Claude once told me he was going to leave the district financially in the same shape he found it and no better off. When I left in 2004 the district had 11 million dollars in the bank. The community thought he was a great financial wizard. Actually the district was in good shape but there was a cost. For a number of years the district received at least one-half a million every spring from the state. It doesn't take a wizard not to spend it. But over this period of time to have this much money what did the students have to lose and for how long. Until the new high school was built that took an extra vote of the people, not much was spent on the school and/or the students in trying to give them an education and getting them ready for life itself. The new building was not Claude's idea in the first place. He only wanted to build additional rooms on the building that is now the middle school. Mr. William Thorpe said he would rather build a new high school than to put rooms on an old building. The board disregarded Claude's plans for additional rooms and moved to look into the possibility of a new school.

MOVING TOWARDS CHANGE???

Change was now starting to take place and the future looked bright for the students of Standish-Sterling. The voters approved the bond for a new high school and upgrades on the other three buildings to everyone's surprise. It was an organized effort of hard work around the community. Mr. Claude Foot's involvement was like it was a few years before on a new track around the football field. Mr. Rick Weizoon told Claude to stay out of the proposal and he would get it passed. So, that is exactly what he did. The proposal passed as long as Mr. Foot said very little. Mr. Foot was not liked in this district to say the least. He would stay the same for the new school. When it passed it was a great day for Standish-Sterling but for me things only got worse. Instead of retiring Mr. Foot now had something to do instead of playing with his personal portfolio every day on school time.

A few years before the bond issue passed I had been taking a look at and reading books on a new type of schedule schools in our conference were going to instead of the traditional class schedule. I was taking teachers and students to different schools that had block scheduling in place. I also sent my new Assistant Principal, Mr. Mark Burger, out with teams of teachers to study what it was like and come back with a recommendation. The echo was sounding one day while Mr. Foot called me to come to his office. I took my time but I went over anyway. As soon as I walked in the door of his office he started bitching about block scheduling and told me he was opposed to it and to quit going and sending anyone to schools that had it. I told him there were many advantages to the block instead of the tradition schedule but he was adamant about being against our district ever going to the block form of scheduling. Any thought of a new schedule was out the door and there was very little I could do or say to get him to change his mind. Again, I was not a happy camper because I knew the advantages our students could have over the schedule the district had.

The block schedule could give the students a chance for taking an additional class and the Seniors might have something they could take and not wasting their time. With the traditional schedule many students wanted and needed more classes. Our top students had very little to choose from because they were beyond what most of our courses covered. They were bored to death. It also provided us with the opportunity of our students getting better prepared for all the new state tests they were taking. It worked at are career center in Bay City and I was hoping we were finally on the move. It was not something a school district can just jump into because new teaching methods would have to be learned by the staff and actually change the way teachers at Standish-Sterling taught over the past thirty or more years. This would be my greatest challenge ahead. But at this point the issue was dead in the water. I always hated water and kept reading and studying the block type of schedule on my own time. I did not see myself staying at Standish-Sterling much longer if things didn't change for the better.

Mr. Burger stayed on for about a year and found another job in southern Michigan when Mr. Foot called me over to his office. I was wondering what the hell now. To my total surprise he asked me why we were not using the block schedule in the school. This was a good two years after he killed the project. I had to tell him he killed it more than two years ago because he wanted no part of it.

At this point I finally figured out Mr. Claude L. Foot. He actually had no idea about what was taking place in the schools. I could not get an answer out of him until the cow jumped over the moon for the second time. The reason he would not ever give anyone an answer wasn't because he had to think about it. He actually had to check everything out with his wife, Kris, who was an administrator at Ogemaw Heights High School in West Branch and a NEMC conference member. Looking at Mr. Foot's background in education I should have known this long before now. He went to Aquinas College until he was asked to leave and switched to Eastern Michigan in Grand Rapids and graduated with a B. S. Degree in Mathematics with an MBA in Business. He taught math for a short time and moved to the Central Office as the business manager and then superintendent of Ecorse, Michigan. The people I knew wanted him out long before he finally left for Standish-Sterling.

I had played cards usually every Friday night with Claude and his wife along with other friends for a few years. Claude finally quit playing because he could not stand to lose a dime. But his wife still played until many of them died over the years. I always felt sorry for his wife knowing what Claude was doing behind her back but I never said a word. She was always the one everyone liked. She was intelligent and had the knowledge Mr. Foot never had in education. She was calling the shots at Standish-Sterling and I think she knew it. Claude was in his own world and nobody could figure him out until it finally all made sense.

I gave Chris a call and asked her how things were going at West-Branch Ogemaw Heights. She said things were going quite well and they were looking at a new type of student schedule. At this point I just played dumb and let her explain what they were doing. It sounded like she was a big believer in block scheduling and told me we should take the time and look into it. I told her we had been thinking about it and would take her advice. I did not explain her husband had shut it down a few years before and never wanted me to bring it up again.

So I got my ducks in order and began setting up teacher committees to check things out once again. I was a big believer in some sort of block scheduling for years. The form of block a school would finally establish depends on the educational institution one was talking about. It had to meet the needs of the school and offer more benefits for the students than the old tradition schedule Standish-Sterling had for far to long. But the stage was now set again and I was ready to help bring SSC into a new and exciting period of time in their history. West-Branch Ogemaw Heights was also looking at a block for a new schedule. It was finally adopted by them and they were off and running. Shortly thereafter Mr. Foot changed his mind and wanted it at Standish-Sterling. He had listened to his wife and now knew the many advantages to a block schedule instead of the traditional one that SSCHS was working with. I thought he was losing his mind. He did not like any part of a block schedule and would not listen to me. Now he was wondering why we did not have one in place yet. The man was not all there.

So I did what I was told to do once again. I wanted to tell him to stick it up his ass. But,

I was loyal and just let it go as in the past. The district was long over due for a change that was needed. I again started taking teachers and students for visits to other schools that had made the change to some form of block schedule. I even invited staffs to SSCHS to talk to my staff about what they encountered and if they preferred the block or not. The teachers knew how I felt about the change now it was my task to convince the staff. I knew the staff quite well by this time and I could tell who would be for the change and not before we started forming a block schedule fitting our needs.

Each and every block schedule is different and must be bought by the staff. I knew I needed at least 75% of the entire high school staff behind me to make the switch a positive one for all. I knew the English department would put up my greatest battle because they were set in their ways and did not change anything for the last thirty years. So, I concentrated on the other departments and it worked.

I had my assistant principal (Mr. Mark Wills) take a straw vote when I thought the time was right. Only two teachers voted to stay the same as it was while everyone else were convinced that a change would be better. This meant the teachers would have to change their methods of teaching to make it work. I would have to monitor their teaching and help in whatever way I could. The vote was well beyond the 75% I needed to switch. My assistant was actually selected by Judah and myself. He was a business teacher in the system and seemed to be quite supportive of me or at least that's what I thought. I even had Mark present the information to the Board because I knew two individuals now on the Board would not favor a change and a new idea. They were the retired union president

Mrs. Harmond and a local vet, Dr. Ron Shob. He never liked me from the day I took the job because I took my dog business to Pinconning, Michigan and a vet that was a personal friend who never tried to rip me off. Dr. Shob wanted to start my dogs on shots as if they had never had one. He did not know I was the only taxpayer in Adams Township who purchased a license for their dogs and they were up to date with their shots. We always argued about the rabies shot and who would accept the ones I gave my hounds. I had twelve hounds at the time and Dr. Shob wanted the money. I know the state of Michigan says a licensed vet had to give the rabies but that wasn't my argument. My friend in Pinconning gave shots to all my dogs. I still take my dogs to him even now.

At this time I knew why they were on the Board and for one reason only. They wanted to get Mr. Foot and I at any cost. Mrs. Harmond even made a statement out loud in Pamida (a local department store) and heard by a school bus driver. The bus driver told me he hated Mrs. Harmond but he said he was in Pamida when she made the comment. At the time they only had two votes against us but they would never give up until we were both gone. I believe Dr. Shob was ready for a nervous breakdown over the situation. He became so obsessed with getting us his oldest son told him to give it up or he was going to leave their business.

One of the first things his son did when he joined his father's practice was to fire his own mother. Tell me they were not all screwed up. I blame the father for the condition his family was in. His daughter was a close friend of mine and even invited me to her graduation party. She was a great student who always came to my office just to talk and eat some candy. I always had candy for the students and myself. I have been an insulin dependent diabetic for over 36 years and kept the candy for emergency situations for me and other student diabetics in school. His daughter was the valedictorian of her class and later became a teacher. It must have been because of my influence on her. She was fantastic even with a father whom I still think is totally out of his head (A real crazy professional in deed). His middle son who I enjoyed the most out of his three children was the one he hated me so much for? Doc even made that remark at a school meeting one afternoon. Jeff was giving him some trouble at home at the time like most children will. Doc could not handle it and wanted to blame someone other than his son himself or by taking a good honest look in the mirror. In my opinion he drove his son nuts but still blamed me for what he became. His son did not aspire to his father's wishes and fought him every step of the way. Doc said he came into the office when this son was a Sophomore for help and I sent him to see a counselor who had the contacts but Doc thought he was no help and never came back to see me about what help he needed at the time. But, he had to blame someone and I became the person without ever knowing it. It's hard enough to raise children today. Two out of three is not bad. The third one was his own man. He chose not to become what his father wanted him to be and this drove the Doc nuts. Instead of blaming himself, as people do not do he blamed me for his second son not reaching his potential. To be honest he should look back and see when his son started drinking and using drugs. Let me just say that his oldest son was not innocent either. His influence on his younger brother might have something to do with it. You can be the judge but blaming me was just crazy. My son is a very successful CPA in Chicago who today has 3.5 million in the bank. But I never forced him to become something his heart wasn't in. He made decisions himself and I could never be more proud of what he became. Who knows someday his middle son will become the man he wants to be. If and when he does it will not be because of his father always being on his butt. In my opinion he is a better person than even his father realizes.

Another factor I believe set his second son apart was his friends he started hanging around with. He hung with a bad group. This group at the time meant more to him than his own family. Doc should have been more concerned about their influence on his son long before he started hounding him constantly. I lived through the same thing when I was young. The best thing I ever did was telling my friends I was done with them and I wanted to make something of myself. This is a hard thing to do but it had to be done. As the group the youngest son was hanging with became more influential than Doc ever realized. He should have talked with his son's friends and told them not to hang with his son or else, if his son was out of control. It can be done because my mother did it while raising five brats by herself. As his son got older the drugs became even harder especially after high school A person is a product of his or her environment and his friends were bad so what chance did he have. It's like trying to quit drugs by hanging with drug dealers. It just doesn't work. Moving away doesn't work either because the kids find the same type of influence they are trying to break away from. His son needed a role model outside his immediate family that cared about his son. I'm not saying I could have been the one but Doc never talked to me about his situation. He just blamed me for his son turning out like he did. His son and I are still very close and we were always friends. I think I would have been the role model and friend his son needed. I do not believe this need ever goes away and I would help him today if I was asked. I do believe the father quit trying to help his son. We had another and more experienced counselor at the school who would have helped him greatly. He never talked to her about his son's problem either. Like I said before, he never talked to me about the problems his son was having. He only had to blame someone and it was I. Even though the boy's father was responsible for what happens to me later in this book he only took half the credit and/or blame. He told me this himself. He said Joan Harmond was the other half.

My once dear friend was just used by them while he was trying to save his own butt. This person was Claude Foot. This is why I will call him Judah from now on. Judah saved himself by turning on Jesus that led to his death on the cross. I am not saying I am God but his action was the same. To this day and from all my teaching and reading the entire Bible I do not believe God ever forgave Judah for what he did to his only son. I do not believe God will ever forgive Claude (Judah) for what he did to me. I know Judah went to see the movie "Passion" but it too never influenced him. I am a believer who is concerned with everyone and not myself. I know I will one day be with the Lord and my mother in heaven. Sometimes I even look forward to it.

I was never afraid to die let alone be afraid of anyone or anything on God's earth. I believe we all have a life after our short stay on Earth and for some of us it will be better than we have now. I'm not crazy and/or stupid I just believe in what I believe.

As it all worked out a block schedule was put together by the staff and myself. It gave the students what they needed at the time. A year later I again had my assistant principal take a survey of the teachers and students. Both groups favored the block schedule by 95% for and 5% against. I was happy for the students and staff and things were going great.

Chapter IX

JUDAH'S CAPERS

BLACKTOP

I was sitting in Mr. Foot's office talking about nothing special when his phone rang. He and I were the only two in his office and his phone was on laud speaker. At the time he let it go and I listened to the whole conversation about to take place between Judah and a local dentist, Ben Brown. I had a feeling because I could hear the echoes all morning. So I turned on my cassette recorder just in case.

Ben started the conversation by asking Judah what was he going to do? Judah said what the hell are you talking about? I thought for a moment Judah was going to ask me to leave but he did not. Ben said people were asking him about the blacktop put around his dental business. People were wondering how much it had cost and who put it in. He said he did not know how to answer them. At this point I was in the dark and didn't know what they were talking about. I knew my answer was forthcoming as I sat there in silence. At this point I checked the recorder and it was working. Remember, I always carried the recorder since my conversation with Father Bob paid off. Judah said you dumb ass to Ben and told him to just do what the rest of us did. He told him the rest of them used paper and prepared a bill from Pyramid Construction out of Saginaw and sign it paid in full. Ben then asked Judah how much he should put down on the bill? Judah told him to find out from someone about how much it cost them to have the blacktop put down around the same square footage as his office took. Ben said OK to Judah and thanked him for his help. The conversation was over and Ben hung up. Judah and I did not say a word to each other about Ben's call and concluded our conversation and I left his office.

I could not believe what I had just heard. I was at the school board meeting and the board voted to resurface the exiting parking lot of the Junior-Senior High School building and add a new part to make in larger. I thought the company would be busy all week doing the parking lot for athletic events. I kept looking out my office window wondering when Pyramid was going to get started. They said they would be in the area all week. As the week progressed I notice the blacktop company was all over the town. It seemed as though Pyramid was so busy everywhere. They were on the move but not at the school. I thought that was a little funny so I kept looking around when I traveled through Standish. A person would have to know how Judah operated. This was something I knew for a number of years. Judah would not do anything without checking it out with his friends. He spent a lot of time on the phone when he was not working on his personal portfolio everyday. He would check with Rick, Jim and Lenny Lubare before moving forward. Len was a local chiropractor and member of the board. Rick Weizoon was a funeral director responsible for getting the votes needed to build a new track and Jim Polls was the one who talked the board into hiring Judah in the first place. While I was driving around Standish I noticed Pyramid laying blacktop either at the home and/or businesses of these individuals. I did not think much about it until Ben made his call to Mr. Foot. Then I checked with the district's bookkeeper, Janice Yenior to see if these individuals ever paid the district for the blacktop done. Janice stated the district paid for the blacktop with one check. In fact the local sheriff told me Jim Polls had blacktop work done by Pyramid during the same time as the rest. The sheriff seemed to know what had taken place and never did anything. He still did nothing when I told him what I knew along with the conversation I was a witness to.

The one who gained the most was the Superintendent himself. He has a driveway that is very long but that was just the beginning. He had his entire backyard and pole building taken care of. I could easily turn a school bus around in the space. Judah was a smart man who never acted more foolishly on this project. He had the company stop black topping his driveway when people could see it from the road. Years later and before he retired he had the project finished as it was connected to the road. I've always wondered who paid for that connection to the road? I have my suspicions though. It had to be done before he retired and it was. Now I was sure what had taken place. Once blacktop is put down it has to be recoated at least every three to four years. This was also done to all the blacktop laid down by Pyramid and for the above-mentioned individuals. That makes them candidates for prosecution. Because this was paid for with school funds. I did try talking to Ben because we were both members of Standish Kiwanis and I was hoping he got involved in this caper accidentally. I thought Judah might have called him and said he ordered too much blacktop and it would be going to waiste if he did not take some. But the more I thought about it the more I was sure that did not happen. I don't think Pyramid lays blacktop on dirt without properly getting the ground ready, staked out and leveled before pouring. So it had to be planned out by the individuals involved from the very beginning. They actually ripped off the school district, the State of Michigan and the community. I proceeded to write Ben a letter telling him what I knew to see how he would respond. He wrote me back saying I was hallucinating and didn't know what I was talking about. So I wrote him again. This time he said if I pursue this he would see me in court. I wrote him again and told him to bring it on. I told him I had his conversation with Judah on tape and I was ready. I know taping a conversation without getting the other person's approval cannot be used in court. But it worked with Father Bob and the Bishop and they settled with me soon after. Sometimes a person has to do what he or she has to do and that's that. When I was the President of Standish Kiwanis Judah was the Treasurer, Ben was a longtime member and Lenny was a past President who served before me.

Ben finally wrote me back again and asked me not to contact him again. I did notice that between the letters to Ben, Judah came back from Arizona. I knew Ben was getting scared at this point and must have talked to Judah and that brought him back to Standish. Neither one would ever admit it but I could see the writing on the wall.

With that out of the way I wrote a letter to the FBI in Bay City and to the State Attorney General, Mr. Mike Cox in Lansing. Mike wrote me a letter back saying he thought the local authorities should handle it. I knew it would never happen because Judah had given the former sheriff a job in the school system when he lost his bid for re-election. He was hired as a janitor until he won re-election later. The FBI called and told me he was putting an agent on the case and he would be in touch with me. In another letter to them I explained his agent had done absolutely nothing whatsoever. So I called the agent and told him how I would proceed with the case. He must not have liked what I said because he again ignored the case. I told him if Ben and/or Judah did not admit what they had done he could speak to Janice or Frieda. He could also contact Pyramid and check their records. But the FBI still did nothing. It was like watching a television show where the FBI comes in after the case was solved and the action being over. In my opinion they were all worthless and chose not to do their jobs. The blacktop caper only cost the taxpayers around $50,000.00—$100,000.00. This might have not been enough but I thought it was. I did not want to see anyone go to prison but as Judah would say who cares? When I wrote Ben the letters I tried to get him to make a donation to the school district in the amount of what the blacktop was worth. He refused so I said to hell with him. He only has himself to blame. Nobody had to twist his arm when he took the blacktop or had it sealed at least every three to four years by the school district. He and Judah will have to live with themselves for stealing from the school district. I guess these types of people have no guilt, or self-respect whatsoever. I've known some people who have lied so much they believed the lie themselves. To them it becomes the truth. At this point I can only hope there is a judgment day. If not I will be very disappointed.

If the authorities did their job I believe the issue would have been over. What they would have received is beyond my power to decide. If it ever went to court in the Standish area, it would depend who was hearing the case. One judge on the circuit court should not be on the bench. He was a bad lawyer and a worse judge. If you don't believe me ask anyone who works in the courthouse. They will give you one name who screws cases up one after another. There is no justice in his courtroom. The outcomes only depend on who you are. Even though I tried to get him off my case as I will tell you later he would not dismiss himself and it cost me at least $500,000.00 in lost wages and benefits and I won the case. This will really turn your stomach if you believe in justice at all. I will visit Judge Ron Bergermister later in this book when the time is right.

PARKING PERMITS

After the blacktop was put down school was about to start again. Like always I find it very helpful to meet with all the student body at one time and go over everything with them. If the student handbook changed at all I take more time with these issues so there is no misinterpretation of the new changes in the rules. I will spend the time needed and answer any questions the students might have. Before the above was done I scheduled class meetings with each class to talk with them one class at a time. I'll speak along with my assistant principal and usually two counselors. I'll have the teacher reps for each class and their class officers. The student officers cover the items pertinent to their class like homecoming. Role is taken and anyone who missed will be contacted at a later date so there are no excuses for not knowing what's going on and what is expected from all concerned.

The parking fee was always $1.00 for parking the student's car in the school's parking lot. I had met with the student body and told them how much it would be one dollar. The current student handbook said the same thing one dollar. As the student went off to class Judah met me in the main office. He told me he wanted the parking fee to go up to $15.00 a year instead of the $1.00 we had charged for years. My thought was he wanted to make more money for the blacktop he stole from the school. This increase was not going to come close to what was stolen from the school and I told him I had just told the students and I was not about to change it. He was really pissed but so was I. To charge the students more to help him raise more money was not needed was just putting the screws to the entire student body. Like always I could not hurt the students over this bullshit and refused to raise the amount.

Judah was so upset with me he decided to take the issue to the Board without any input from me or telling me what he was going to do. The meeting with the Board took place before the next Board meeting and it was decided in committee like most things on their agenda are. In Judah's opinion he was the boss and that was that. I usually went along with him if it did not hurt the students. This did and I refused to change. I had my reasons and nobody would ever know but me until now. I know it was a small issue compared to many things in a school but it meant I would lose my self- respect and my word to the students would mean nothing. I have a younger brother, Duane who worked in the GM Plant in Bay City and he heard about what the high school principal had done to the students before the issue was over. I told him I was not the one who wanted to raise the amount but I was taking the heat once again. I could hear the echoes once again.

The next thing I knew was the Board increased the parking fee for one year to $5.00. Like I said above the Board decided to raise the fee based on information Judah gave the Board committee. The committee made a recommendation to the entire Board and it was accepted as presented. The board never asked me what I thought and I guessed they didn't care. Another small but decisive victory for Judah ended up looking like I was the culprit. I had to inform the students and I did without telling anyone the true facts. I had to suck this one up. The way this was handled is usually the way things are determined on many Boards. I know of one district in the state that meets in a local tavern and discusses the agenda before and after the Board meeting. This actually breaks the law but nobody seems to care. This is the type of society we live in or as Board members would say this is how they get things done. Even though it breaks the law on school boards not meeting privately with the majority of Board members nobody says a word. In Standish this was done all the time as it will be done again in my case when I was forced to sue the Board on another matter.

CABLE, CARPET, COMPUTERS & WOOD

No matter what happened in the school district Judah would always get something for himself out of it. It was like he had to get something even if he had to steal it like the Athletic Directors hat at the conference golf outing. Nothing ever took place good and/or bad he did not take care of himself first and foremost. This was one of his baby traits he never got over.

When Channel One was putting in the cable to the then Junior and Senior High school building he had them cut the cable and run it to his house. As of today May 30, 2011 he still has it running to his house and he pays nothing. This has gone on for twenty years or so at no expense to him. The school district has covered the costs of providing this service. The cable takeoff can be seen from Grove Road, running to a utility pole and from there into his house.

I have Direct TV and pay around $70.00 each month for my service. I have a dish in my backyard the cable is attached to and from there into my house. This is around $840.00 per year: times 20 or $16,800.00 of free cable over this period of time with the taxpayers paying the bill. I have gone to all the Board meetings for eighteen years and the Board (s) over the years has never voted on this service. I would say they were never aware of what was happening. I know it was never in his contract with the district either. This is just another one of Judah's rip-offs costing the district and taking funds away from the students. Was this a man who always put the interest of the children first? You can be the judge.

During another year Judah had new carpeting put in the band room at the old high school. After it was installed he decided he did not like the line going across the room and had the carpet replaced. I was visiting him one day at his house and noticed the new band carpeting that was taken out of the high school band room was installed down his basement from wall to wall. I guess this was another gift given to him by the district and the Board? What do you think? I know what I think and know.

For the many years I worked for the district Judah would get a new computer at least every six months. He would take them apart all the time and put them back together. He was getting very good at this task. I never knew what happened to his older computers until I was at his house again seeing his pole barn. He had a large number of computers in his barn bought by the district sitting on a new wooden work bench that use to be the gym floor at one time. I think you get the picture.

I sent the local authorities out to take a look at all the above. I had told this person not to check with the sheriff and he told me he didn't. Months later he got back to me saying the local prosecutor told him the statute of limitations had passed and even if these things happened he could do nothing about it because it was beyond seven years since it happened. I told him I knew the law but he was wrong. I told him it was like the blacktop. Because the district paid for the re-surfacing of the blacktop every three to fours years it still comes under the statute (law). The same thing would be for the cable. It is still being provided for and paid by the district. He said I was most likely right and he would get back to me. I'm still waiting because I know I will never get an answer. Like the sheriff Judah gave the prosecutor's wife a job in the school district. I knew I was at a dead end on these issues along with the blacktop. If the school district is content with what and who is getting these things I would also like to be provided with the same free service for my eighteen years of working for the district and getting shit on in the end. In fact, I believe everyone in the district should be getting the above items free of charge. Judah is no better than the rest of us in fact he and his wife are a little less in my book. You can form your own opinion because what I have stated is the truth. Just for your information I am the President elect of a group called WMW TRUTH. It's an international organization that believes in living and telling the truth no matter what the outcome ends up being. This is a hard thing to always do but I never tell a lie. I have other weaknesses but this is not one of them. I can be reached at dogman2@sch-net.com if you want to be a lifetime member. I will send you a lifetime card for $10.00 and your name will be added to the list of members.

SICK AND VACATION DAYS

After the second year Judah was Superintendent of Schools in Standish-Sterling he was given the opportunity to write his own contract by the then Board President, Patricia Schmidt. She seemed to only be interested in getting the non-certified people in the district. I could never understand this because her older sister was one of them. This group consisted of secretaries, janitors, aids and bus drivers. So she was not concerned about what Judah had in his contract. It was a three-year contract normal for superintendents in the area. All the other school administrators only had a two-year contract without any of the added benefits Judah gave himself. The benefits I knew about were his life insurance policy; having the district pay his 7% Social Security; getting the cash value of his Blue cross-Blue Shield Plan because he was covered by the West Branch-Rose City Schools because his wife worked for them; and a sick and vacation day plan that was super. This part of his contract stated if the district ever wanted him gone they would have to pay him an additional three years with all his benefits. He had this at the district he came from and the amount paid for his home in Standish. The sick and vacation portion of his contract stated all his unused days each year would accumulate and when he left the district for any reason the district would have to pay him at his rate of pay he was working for. When he finally decided to retire the district owed him well beyond $375,000.00. He would receive around $500.00 per day times thirty-two days a year times the number of years he worked for the district about 24 years. This would make it $384,000.00. No other employee would ever come close to that amount when they retired. If he was fired he would receive an additional $375,000.00 on top of $384, 000 or $759,000.00 in total. I was given a copy of a letter to the Board Judah wrote stating if they do not back off on trying to get him he was also going to sue them for a lot more based on his average evaluations he received each year. This was why the Board backed off on firing him on at least three different occasions. I remember one time when the Board President sent a copy of his contract out to the district lawyers wondering how the Board could break it. The district lawyer told the Board to back off because it was iron clad. I thought it was not good practice for only the Board President to ever see his contract even though it was public information anyone in the district had a right to see. This was just like my yearly evaluations. They become public information but nobody seemed to care at the time. When the Board President sent Judah's contract out he forgot to tell the attorney to send his reaction back to him at his home address. As you might guess Judah received the school's attorney opinion in the school's mail and I thought he was going to have a heart attack on the spot. Two things followed right after Judah opened his mail. The President of the Board resigned from the Board and Judah fired the attorney. I can see why he did both of these things. It wasn't a smart thing to do by the Board President. I thought the attorney should have called Judah but that wasn't done and his firm was fired. Judah then hired a friend out of Grand Rapids to become the district's attorney and he was loyal only to Judah. Years later the Board hired the old firm back that actually knew something about school law. For a number of years every Board that came about wanted Judah out and a few years later the Board tried again.

Judah did something all his administrators knew about. He would take a few weeks off to go golfing every year. He went to Georgia and Florida with a group of around twenty golfers from the Standish-Sterling Area. Being his second in command he always put me in charge of the district when he was gone. I never had a problem when he was out of town. Judah stated many times he left the district in good hands and he knew I could handle whatever came up.

After two years of Judah going south with the guys the group told him they did not want him on the trip anymore because he was driving many of the guys nuts. I can only imagine. One friend of mine told me a story as to why he could not stand him. Judah was a good golfer but he always told the others on the trip how to do it even if they did not want the help. This friend of mine Mr. Gary Schwartz bought a set of Ping golf clubs to improve his game and scores. It was quite expensive from what I was told by Gary. One day he and Judah were going up in the hotel elevator and Judah told Gary he was nuts to spend that kind of money when he was a shitty golfer in the first place. I know Gary wanted to kill him at this point. Judah ended up saying these types of things to many of the local golfers and as a group they were pissed. So they told him he was no longer wanted.

As things worked out he started to go South and golf with the only one that would go with him his wife Christine. Boy did I feel sorry for her. Judah had a sense of humor nobody found funny. He was no PR man for the district and just about everyone in the community hated him. This was why I always wondered how he could keep his job year after year. After a few years I knew. He actually blackmailed most of them and his contract was binding and could not be broken. Believe me the Board tried. At one point the Board meetings became a laughing joke. No matter what was said Judah and the Board disagreed. I'm sorry to say with all this Board pressure Judah finally had a heart attack in his doctor's office that was connected to the hospital in Standish. He then took a few weeks off again and he put me in charge while he recovered. Until this point in my life I never wished Judah anything bad. I was extremely loyal to him and at this point his only friend. I understood what he lived through and felt sorry for him most of the time. He understood money and that was as far as it went. Even though we did not see things the same way I covered his behind more times than I could say. For my loyalty to Judah I could see things in the district changing for the worst again. Judah had nowhere to turn after a while but he was ready to retire at this point in his career.

This was the time Judah and my relationship changed drastically. He was blaming me for things I had nothing to do with and then making me walk the plank for him on everything he did wrong instead of listening to what I had to say. I knew I was now his target but I never believed it in my heart. I know I should have trusted my instincts more than I did but I believed in people and did not change my self-respect and my belief in honesty would always prevail.

CHAPTER X

BAPTIZED IN DIRTY WATER

THE ULTIMATE BETRAYAL

The high school had been running better than ever. Improvements have been made along with a new high school and student schedule. The block was put into effect with a 95% or more rating by the staff and student body. MEAP scores improved from 75% to 79.6% in one year. What more could be asked?

Then, I received a call after school was out by Judah's secretary. She asked me if she had called before and I said no not in a while. She said there was a meeting scheduled with me and the Board committee in Judah's office at 7:00 a.m. the next day. I asked her what it was about and she said she did not know. I knew she was hiding something but did not want to say. I decided to call Judah and find out about the meeting. Judah said he was too busy to meet with me and he could not say what the meeting was about but he wanted me there. I told him I would see him in the morning and our conversation came to an end.

The echoes had been sounding in my ears for a few days and I had a feeling something was not right. I have always met the students every morning as they entered the building. A few days before I was standing in my usual position when the choir director Mr. Hadaway joined me. I could tell he wanted to say something he knew but didn't know how to tell me. He finally asked me if I knew what was going on. I told him I had a suspicion but actually didn't know a thing.

I knew he was a good friend of Dr. Ron Shob who was on the Board. Dr. Shob was the one who blamed me for his middle child who didn't meet with his expectations of what Doc wanted him to be. The choir instructor finally could not hold his information in any longer. He told me a few Board members had been meeting on getting rid of me no matter what the cost. I said it sounded like Joan Harmond when she was in Pamida and the bus driver heard her and told me about it. So I played dumb and said nothing but I knew he was telling the truth.

Before this happened a few friends of mine told me four to five members of the Board had meetings at Dave and Kathy's restaurant in Sterling and they were talking about me. They said they would testify in court for me because their meetings were illegal and not right. So I was aware of what was going on without the choir director's input. But that just told me other people knew if he did. Word was spreading like a wild fire. In a small community things get around quickly. I must have been the talk of the town because people are that way.

The next thing I did was to tell my wife and mother what was taking place. It was no surprise for my wife because I always told her everything. My mother was another story. She was getting up there in age and actually suffered enough in her life. She was so proud of her five children and what they had all accomplished in life it gave her a reason to live. Now, her heart was saddened once again. Telling her what was about to happen was the hardest thing I ever had to do in my life. We had a bond that could not be any tighter but from that day on I kept her informed along with Gloria, my wife.

The next day I walked into the meeting and just decided to listen and not get upset over anything said. A few months before the school administrators were having a meeting in Judah's office when his secretary came in and said there were three Board members of the Board in the office and they wanted to look through the administrators files. Judah hesitated for a few seconds and told her it would be fine. He stated this was a public school and the public had the right to look into employee's files. Years ago he would have made a big deal about this but this time he let it go. He was no idiot and knew his butt was in trouble with the majority of Board members at the time. The teachers she served as president put our ex-teacher who was now retired on the Board. They could control at least four-five hundred votes at the polls. The schools were running so smoothly the association controlled the votes for a number of years. As I have pointed out many times teachers could get away with anything at Standish-Sterling and nobody seemed to care. Joan Harmond was now on the Board and she became the president a year or two later. She did not stop there. She had talked one of her classmates from her school years to run for the Board and her friend were also elected. Dr. Ron Shob ran for the Board when the voter turnout was extremely low. I had tried to talk a few of my friends to run against him but they said no. Dr. Shob received 21 votes and was elected to the Board. Later he talked a friend of his into running for the Board, Mr. Jack Snowfield, and he was also elected to the Board. This gave the group a majority of voting members now serving on the local school board. They picked up another member who was elected to the Board shortly thereafter.

Mr. Dave Sondberg who I thought was a good friend of mine also turned against me. He was a good friend of our local sheriff and his wife. The sheriff and his wife still wanted my ass for talking to his youngest daughter that Judah set me up for a while back. Now with Judah running like a scared rabbit something was about to change. Judah was their first target and I knew I was going to be next in line. What I did not count on was Judah protecting his ass by giving me up. I knew I should have taken either of the jobs offered to me just before this meeting took place. Like Joan the ones I have just mentioned had their own agenda that was the same as Joan's. She was a bitter woman who had a terrible life and wanted mine to be the same.

Just about everyone in the community thought Judah and I were friends long before we both took a job at Standish-Sterling because I was the first administrator he hired. We knew we had a lot of work to do in trying to get Standish-Sterling into the 21st century and we worked together doing it. We golfed in the same league for many years and we bowled on the same team for over ten years. I can see why the community thought the way they did. Whenever we went to a game I drove and we went together. Once a week we would play cards with six to eight others in the community until many of them passed in heaven. Now there are only a few of us left from those days. But, I never thought he would turn on me for no reason except to save his own ass and he did. If you call that loyalty on his part you should re-read this book. He was only loyal to himself and did not care about anyone including his spouse.

Before I walked into the meeting I knew what was about to happen with the committee. I was hoping Judah would have something positive to say about me but inside I knew what he would do. We had known each other for the past eighteen years and shared our personal life with each other nobody knows about. For many years I was his only friend he had in the area. We covered for each other on many occasions both professionally and in the community. But all this was now over because he was fighting for his survival.

This is what makes us different. I would always put the welfare of others above myself. This is what I believe in. I remembered the days I was working at Bay City All Saints and the community and Board wanted me to replace my head football and basketball coach. This was the same person. I told the Board I thought he was one of the best coaches I had ever worked with. His record was not the best but that was not to blame. We were a small class D school and we had to play class A & B schools for two years or until the signed contracts were done and this is what we did. I told the Board if they wanted me to fire this man they would have to get me first because I was not going to do it. When I left All Saints at the end of my second year. This man and many others walked out shortly after I did. This is what I call true loyalty and not the fake loyalty most people adhere to. I have always viewed loyalty as a two way street. To receive loyalty one must give it. From my experience loyalty usually stops if money is involved or either party does not show it. I can honestly say I have been loyal unless it meant breaking the law like Judah did before.

For years I listened to Judah saying to always cover your ass. He made sure he always did and kept a record of exactly what. For some reason he thought I had a record on him and even asked me about it many times over the years. I told him to trust me because he knew me so well he knew I would never turn on him first. This was one thing I never did. If I disagreed with what he was doing I would always tell him and never let anyone else hear about our disagreement. I told Judah I had a file on everything that went by my office. I knew he did not like it but he taught me to do it from the first day I met him. It seemed to be OK for him to do it but not me and I think by now you know why. But, I never had a list or record on him that would hurt him in any way, shape or form. Everything was in my head. I never forget a thing. A few times in my career I had to record what was being said for my own protection and I did along with some photos I still possess.

I remember information was getting to Judah before I did anything. I knew I had a snitch in the closet and I worked out a plan to find out who it was. There were only two individuals I shared my thoughts with and I knew it had to be one of them. I put down a bunch of letters and numbers on my computer that meant nothing at all and left my computer running. My assistant principal Mark Wills saw what was on my computer and asked me what it was. He thought it had to be in some sort of code that only I knew. The other person who saw the numbers and letters said nothing about what he saw and went on and did his job. A few days passed and I found out who was stabbing me in the back. Judah asked me what I had on my computer that was coded. I told him it was nothing at all and nothing was ever coded or listed. I told him to take a look if he wanted to and I thought that was that. I did not tell him I now knew who was the rat because

Judah and my assistant were trying to get something on me but they never did because there was nothing to get. When I was with Mark he never said a good word about Judah and I truly believe he hated the way Judah administered the school system. He told me he thought I was a great high school principal and the Board should go after Judah and not me. He said he could not believe what the Board was doing but there was nothing he could do about it. He didn't know by this time I knew better. It seemed as though I was working with a bunch of people who were honestly baptized in dirty water.

I could not trust any one of them and I did not. Knowing all the above I walked into the meeting not knowing what to expect.

FIRST AND ONLY MEETING

When I entered Judah's office and sat down for the meeting that was about to start I saw the following people; Judah, the Curriculum Director, Mr. Roger Sanderson, Dave and Joan Harmond. Mrs. Viginia Bacowski was not there yet. So we had to wait a few minutes and nobody said a word. When she arrived the meeting began. Joan started the meeting by saying I would not be the high school principal next year. I asked her why not? She had no answer and went on from there. She went through a bunch of BS stating what a great job I had done over the years I had been a principal but the committee decided it was time to make a change. She asked me how many years I had been the Principal here at Standish-Sterling. I told them I had been at SSCHS for eighteen years. Dave spoke up and said eighteen years was a long time and wanted to know how long all together. It was like I was being interviewed for the first time. I told the committee I had been a high school principal for 32 years and had 34 years in education altogether. Dave said he thought that was long enough and said the board committee wanted me to take another position. I did not say a word at this point and let them go on. Joan said they didn't want to hurt me and they were thinking about a new administrative position but it hadn't been worked out yet. She asked me if I would be interested in it or not? I told them I was getting a little older and depending on the position itself I would think about it. I think my answer threw them off guard. They expected me to get mad and throw a fit but I was as relaxed as I could be and asked them what they were thinking about. They had no idea but they said I was good for the district and my relationship with the student body was second to none. Joan said if I was interested they would set up a meeting in a few weeks and they would tell me what they would come up with. Joan said it would be a position with the same pay and benefits I was already making. She stated I already had a two-year contract for the future and they wanted me to do something with the district in the line of public relations or things of that sort. I told them I was not planning on looking for another job at this point and once they figured out what this new position was I would meet with them and go over it. Mrs. Bacowski said if I didn't want the new position I could stay as the high school principal for as long as I wanted. Joan disagreed and said again my tenure as principal was done and gave Virginia a dirty look. At this point I knew they were not all together on making this move or Virginia was out in left field on her own. I thought they should have had the new position worked out somewhat before they met with me about moving to a new job they absolutely had no idea what they wanted or needed. In my opinion they were jumping the gun. But, I told them I would think about it and meet with them in the near future. Like I thought Judah never said a word at this meeting. I think he felt ashamed at what he was part of but didn't want to makes waves for himself. He was not running the show like he had in the past and just sat there like a dead skunk he was. I left the meeting and went back to my office and got ready to meet with the staff because it was a conference day for the teachers and I had a few things to get ready. They asked me not to say anything yet but give it some thought. I told them the entire staff was waiting to hear what this meeting was all about and I had to tell them something and left.

I walked into the high school building and around ten staff members were waiting for me and wanted to know what happened at the big meeting. I didn't say anything to the group because I wanted some time for myself. I did tell them we were going to have an In- Service Day and I still had things to finish before our meeting. I knew the staff wanted to know what was happening but I needed the time to think how I was going to tell them. My assistant principal came into my office and I told him what happened. I also told him to be ready to run the In-Service Day because I had to see my wife and mother and tell them what was taking place. I did not want to tell them on the phone but I had things to do before I could leave for the day.

Mark said he could not believe what they were doing. But, I knew better. He was the thorn in my side and wanted my position even though I knew he was not ready.

Mark would miss two to three days every week and never report his absence to the central office. I even called the central office at different times to see if he turned the days in and they always said no. I had talked to Judah many times about what he was doing but as usual Judah didn't care and didn't want to get involved. Judah never liked conflict and always tried to get someone else to do his dirty work. One guess as to who that person was. Like a fool I always did what I was told because I was an extremely loyal employee who still trusted Judah to a point. Now I knew better. While he was now fighting for his life he could not be trusted at all. I could see the staff wanted to know what happened in Judah's office. The Board members got the information out long before the meeting was ever scheduled. The Choir Director told me Dr. Shab told him because they were good friends. Ron Shab was not even on this committee but he stood with them behind the scenes. He was even at the illegal secret meetings this committee had at Dave's restaurant along with Virginia, the Sheriff and his wife, Traci and Dave.

I told the staff what happened at the meeting in Judah's office. I told them their ex-president of their association told me I would not be the high school principal next year no matter what. I told them I could see the little smile on her face when she told me. Because she was still involved with the teaching staff and an active member of their Association I knew the staff would not say much as a group. I realized a long time ago there was not a member of the staff that would fight the association. Teachers in the district ran the district and that was the way it was. They played the community like a game of cards when they were dealing from the bottom of the deck. One member on the staff always told me he would be behind me if I ever decided to fight Judah out in the public. I never did because I knew this person would be so far behind me he could not be found and I was right. Whatever the association wanted the staff supported.

I remember one time years ago when my assistant principal admitted to his wife he was having an affair. I knew something was going on because the women he was having the affair with was his secretary who worked with him on attendance. This person was the one person who worked with me for over thirteen years. It was Denny II. I noticed they were both losing a tremendous amount of weight and each had to buy new clothes something was wrong in Denmark. The problem for me was his wife was on my staff. Sue was a great English teacher who I hired a few years before. Until Denny II told her, she had no idea as to what was going on or with his secretary. The shit was about to hit the fan.

One afternoon towards the end of the school year I received a call at the staff luncheon asking me to hurry back to the high school because something happened. Arriving at school I realized something was definitely on the rise. Another of my secretaries came running over to me and said Sue and Darci got into a fight in the office and they were both upset. I wanted to take immediate action before someone was going to die. I separated the two women and talked to each one individually. Sue, Denny II's wife was in denial and said Darci started the fight. She explained how Darci approached her from behind and started beating on her for no reason. I later talked to Darci and she explained it started just the opposite of what Sue stated. Neither one would back down and I knew someone was not telling the truth. Because Sue was a member of my teaching staff the association and Mrs.

Harmond stood on her side. After Sue told me Darci had no reason for what she did, I knew Sue was telling me one big lie. Sue had every reason to hate Darci and I knew about her temper from what her husband told me about her. This was probably the first item putting Mrs. Harmond and I on opposite sides. Joan Harmond would come into my office every morning right after she became President of her Association. We would sit together for at least one-half to one hour before school started each day for over two months. She told me about her mother who retired from the school district many years ago. Her name was Barmstrong and Joan thought she was the meanest woman on earth. Joan told me so many stories about her mother I realized she did not have a happy childhood because of their relationship. On the other side I had a mother who was the best. I believe this had a lot to do with our relationship. How could anyone hate his or her mother, as much as she did I'll never understand because I was never in her shoes? Joan will have to grow up and not become what she hated her mother for. I have seen this so much I have always wondered why people never learn from those kinds of people instead of becoming just like them. I know my father taught me a lot but the bad things he did would not be found in me and/or my life. I learned what not to do so I would not be like him. It was a battle I have had to fight because this was all I saw and knew. I never said too much with my father around but I was learning all the time. I was learning what not to do.

Joan started our early morning meetings. I knew her purpose was to find something out about Judah or myself she could use against us. I warned Judah about what she was trying to do but he saw it as a weakness in me. He could never be so wrong. I was always trying to cover his back by letting him know what I knew. In his letter to the Board telling them to get off his back or he was going to see them in court stated I was afraid of how the Board would react to whatever I would do but he was all wet. I was just trying to keep him out of harms way time after time. When Joan and Doc Shab got on the Board I told him what to expect next and I was so right. These two were out for one thing but they did not have the majority of votes to do anything. I always figured I worked for Judah and he worked for the Board of seven who knew nothing about nothing. I figured he would watch my back and I would watch his. But as you know a scared rabbit never watches his back let alone someone else's. Judah chose to run and hide like he did in the case of the student with the rifle. He was consistent in his actions and behavior towards any conflict that arose. People who really didn't know him would have thought the opposite but I knew better.

Before I left school for the day I called Gloria and told her I found out what the Board wanted the meeting with me for and I wanted to tell her face-to-face not over the phone. I told my assistant principal he would be in charge of the remainder of the In-Service Day with the teachers and left to go home. I had prepared my wife and mother for what was to come so they knew. I had brought a copy of my last yearly evaluation home with me to show my mother I had been given all superior ratings in every category along with the same marks for the last 17 years. Like everyone else she could not believe what was happening to her boy who was now 57 years old and taken out of his principal position he successfully held for 18 years without giving me a reason for such action. Gloria, my wife, already knew everything and stuck by me like glue. I always said marrying her was the best thing I had ever done. My mother was in the blind and I had to tell her everything. From that day on my mother worried so much about me I still today believe it lead to her death about a year later. We had a special attachment that comes between a mother and son.

A few months later Sue Smith, Denny II's wife, was sticking to her story. Darci finally threatened Sue with an assault charge and Sue finally broke down and told the truth about what happened. Sue had attacked Darci in the office. For her actions Sue had to give up her teaching position within the school system and could not come within so many feet of Darci or she was going to court on assault charges. Needless to say Denny II did not want to be working in the system either. This was when Denny II went out and found another job. He came back a year later because his son was graduating and then he left again and this time for good. For those two years I not only had to do my job as principal I had to do Denny II's. He was letting things go because his heart wasn't in it at least at Standish-Sterling anymore. Judah always said I would be financially compensated for doing both jobs but I never was. Again, not a great surprise.

From that time on Joan and I never worked together. We saw things differently on everything that happened. The battleground was set. It was like putting dogs and cats in the same room with each one being at opposite ends. I tried to do what was right while she seemed to always bring in the association and the battle was taking place. Judah stood with me until his job was on the line and then he turned like a red coat in the Civil War.

Joan really didn't care who she was hurting along the way. I never knew if she ever told the truth on anything.

She had one thing on her mind and that was all. Just for your information, Joan was a cat lover and I raised dogs. I always told the truth and she lied on everything I could think of. I know people sometimes see things differently but this became a joke. She would oppose me on every issue up until she finally won the war. Because of her actions this always put me at the opposite end of the teacher association. I saw the association as a big sore on my foot. It seemed to only protect the weak employees. The better teachers had little to actually do with the association and could care less about what they were doing. Except these same teachers would always take a stand with the association and never oppose it out in the public. Privately, at least in the confines of my office the better teachers stood with me on most every issue but didn't have the guts to stand up as an adult and fight for what they truly believed in. I think this is a major fault with most unions and/or associations. Individuals cannot act independently because they are too afraid. Adults don't believe in themselves and/or their own abilities. Our society seems to be like Judah in that they are running scared and are more consumed with protecting themselves than doing what is right. Children seem to never fear and unlike their adult counter parts are more willing to stand up for what they believe in as the truth. This is the way I think I am. I never want to grow up if it means losing my self-respect and not standing on my own feet and telling the truth no matter what.

WAITING FOR A MEETING

Like the Board committee promised me we would set up a meeting in about two weeks to talk about the new position after they thought about it and what they were going to call it. The Board committee finally came up with the title of Director of Activities for the District. I spent a lot of time thinking about what it meant to me because the district already had a Community Education Director and Athletic Director all in one. His name was Ben Winters. Ben replaced Mr. Thomas Born who had been with the district for at least twenty-five years.

Mr. Born was let go for no particular reason except Ben had been working for the local paper and was looking for a better paying job. The sad thing about what happened to Tom was pure politics. Tom was at least at work everyday while Ben was hard to find. During Tom's last year Judah treated him like he had the plague. Judah sent him down to Standish Elementary School and he sat there and did nothing whatsoever. Tom was later sent to Roger Sanderson's office and Roger had him stuff envelopes for him. Judah heard about what Tom was doing for Roger and he went nuts. He told Roger he did not want Tom to do anything. I believe Judah thought that if Tom did anything at all he might get another contract. I thought it was no way to treat anyone especially an individual who did his job for over twenty-five years and I let my feeling be known to Judah and anyone else who asked. It was demeaning and plain torture for Tom. I knew in my mind Judah was going to treat me the same way he did Tom if I stayed so I told him to forget about it because I was not Tom. My self-respect was still higher than both of them altogether. Whatever self-respect Tom had, Judah made sure he took it away by treating Tom the way he did during his last year. But, I was the only one who really cared and swore it was not going to happen to me. What do you think?

My personal evaluations were fantastic as the high school principal. I believe they speak for themselves. Each one was the highest in the district and pissed off the Board committee I was trying to work with. Here is the last evaluation I had at SSC and it was done in the summer of 2003.

Like I said before, I would put any of my evaluations up against anyone in the district especially Judah himself. When the Board evaluated him, he would barley pass with an average grade. This really pissed Judah off to no end. When a school district has a high school principal doing his or her job all in the superior category it should mean something. Come to find out it meant absolutely nothing. The Board would not talk about it with anyone.

STANDISH-STERLING COMMUNITY SCHOOL
DISTRICT
STANDISH, MICHIGAN 48658
ADMINISTRATIVE EVALUATION
2002-2003
Mr. Dennis Haut

INTRODUCTION

Evaluation is a tool that can be used to increase both the efficiency and effectiveness of an organization. This Administrative Evaluation is intended to help develop consistent administrative procedures and to promote the implementation of a team management concept.

An effective school manager must be skilled in many areas. The responsibilities and duties demand that the administrator demonstrate skill in all areas of management. This evaluation will focus on the following:

Leadership
Motivation
Communication
Interaction/Influence
Problem Solving
Decision Making
Implementing District Procedures
Control Procedures

These categories will be used to generate a composite profile of the administration of this district. The rating scale is as follows:

1 = Superior
2 = Above Average
3 = Average
4 = Poor
5 = Deficient

PROCEDURE

The employee will conduct a self-evaluation. The superintendent will concurrently evaluate the employee. A conference will be held to discuss the data collected. The self-evaluation will be used for discussion purposes only. The final evaluation will be prepared by the superintendent.

LEADERSHIP

This section pertains to the ability of the administrator to assist all staff members in providing their maximum contribution to the organization.

Is respected by and has confidence of staff members. 1

Serves as a role model for all persons with whom they come into contact in their job. 1

Demonstrates respect for policies and procedures of the district. 1

Seeks to use skills and abilities of staff members constructively. 2

Exhibits competence and self-control. 1

Demonstrates ability to organize and implement procedures required to accomplish necessary tasks. 2

Displays cooperative attitude with students, staff, and community. 1

MOTIVATION

This section pertains to the ability of the administrator to encourage staff members to expend the energies required to be successful in their jobs.

Defines realistic expectations for staff members and communicates these expectations to the individuals. 2

Has a positive attitude towards goals and objectives of the district. 1

Provides encouragement and reinforcement for staff members to support them in their jobs. 1

Intervenes, as necessary, to improve marginal performance. 2

Treats all staff members fairly and consistently. 1

Is open and honest in dealings with staff members. 1

Is conscious of the needs of the employees and of their personal and professional goals. 1

Encourages staff members to freely give their maximum effort to the organization. 2

COMMUNICATIONS

This section pertains to the ability of the administrator to manage the flow of information accurately and openly.

Shares information, as appropriate, with staff members. 1

Shares information with fellow supervisors and superintendent. 1

Seeks out the opinions and attitudes of staff members. 2

Implements procedures to improve the accuracy of information. 1

Assure that communication flows through upward, downward, and lateral channels. 1

Provides adequate communication to parents and community regarding school programs and activities. 2

Shares information with staff members through formal communication and/or regular meetings. 1

INTERACTION/INFLUENCE

This section pertains to the abilities of the administrator to establish appropriate relationships with staff members.

Understands administrative role and also relationship of current administrative position to overall operation of the district. 1

Establishes appropriate relationships with staff members. 1

Works together with others to achieve the objectives of the district. 1

Recognizes leadership skills of staff members and uses these skills effectively. 1

Relates with staff members in a manner that provides for a proper blend of authority and support. 2

Places professional responsibilities before personal relationships in dealing with staff members. 1

DECISIONMAKING

This section pertains to the ability of the administrator to outline and implement the appropriate course of action in a given situation.

Makes routine decisions effectively. 1

Seeks consultation on non-routine decisions. 1

Seeks out and uses best available information in decision-making process. 1

Considers long-range implications and outcomes of current decisions. 1

Provides opportunity for input from people affected by decision. 1

Demonstrates fairness in decision-making process. 1

PROBLEM SOLVING

This section pertains to the ability of the administrator to develop and implement solutions to problems.

Considers the implications on all parties involved in the conflict. 1

Places professional responsibilities before personal relationships in dealing with staff members. 1

Analyzes all reasonable alternatives prior to implementing solutions. 2

Considers the priorities of the school district in developing solutions to problems. 1

Seeks assistance, when necessary, in dealing with major problems. 1

Seeks solutions that solve rather than defer problems. 1

INTERPRETING DISTRICT PROCEDURES

This section pertains to the ability of administrators to develop and implement strategies designed to accomplish the educational priorities of the district.

Conducts periodic review of existing programs to insure the best use of district resources. 2

Understands the long-range needs of the students in the district. 1

Clearly communicates expectations to staff members. 1

Anticipates future needs of students and develops methods of implementing programs to meet these needs. 1

Integrates and coordinates activities with other areas of the school district. 2

Respects decisions and directions of the Board of Education and other supervisors. 1

Sets high standards for self, staff, and students. 1

Provides a supportive environment so both staff and students can realize their full potential. 1

Resolves conflicts between organizational and individual expectations. 1

CONTROL PROCEDURES

This section pertains to the ability of the administrator to supervise the day-to-day operations of their area of responsibility.

Implements policies and procedures of the school district. 1

Monitors performance of staff members. 2

Submits necessary reports as required. 1

Explains policies and procedures clearly to staff, students, and community. 1

Effectively utilizes both the physical and personnel talents of the school district. 1

Monitors activities in their building. 1

Intervenes as required to correct inappropriate behavior. 2

Delegates responsibility effectively. 1

Establishes and enforces clearly defined parameters of acceptable behavior. 1

SUMMARY

The following section will include a list of the administrative strengths of the individual. As part of the conference, objectives for the following year will be developed. These will be reviewed periodically and revised as necessary. The employee will also be provided the opportunity to comment about the evaluation.

Strengths

Reliable and gets things done on time and in a professional manner.

An excellent role model for staff and students.

Works hard at establishing good public relations in and for the district.

OBJECTIVES

Design a plan for teachers to cover the state benchmarks in areas tested.

Work with building committee to make sure year two of the high school's accreditation plan for NCA goes positively.

Work with high school steering committee on their school improvement plan to make sure things are being done accordingly.

Dennis J. Haut   Claude L. Foot
                  6/3/03   6/4/03
_____ _____   _____ _____
Employee Signature Date   Superintendent Signature Date

COMMENTS: Signatures are on the original with the above dates.

While I was thinking about this new position Judah called me over to his office. I was thinking this would be the time we went over what the new position would be. I walked into the meeting expecting a least one member of the Board committee but there was none. Roger Sanderson was with Judah as a witness for him. This was something I did on more occasions than I would like to remember. I would sit there but not allowed to say a word. Judah had to say everything if he was right or wrong. So Roger was there to take notes. I was not holding this against Roger because I always thought he was an honest man who would tell the truth. I could not give him a higher compliment. There were not to many in this district I could say that about. Judah didn't know it at the time but Roger would be my witness for what was discussed.

As soon as I sat down Judah wanted to know if I had made up my mind yet. I told him the two weeks were not up yet and before I could give him an answer I wanted to know what the new position was. He told me I could do anything in the district and the position didn't matter. He didn't realize it mattered to me. Remember what I saw Tom Born go through and it was not going to happen to me. Judah actually said I had no choice in the matter and he did not want the Board involved. I told him what the Board committee promised me and I wanted at least

127

one member from that group at this meeting. I could not say yes or no to a job I had no idea as to what it was and/or what the Board wanted me to do. The echoes started rumbling in my stomach and I knew Judah was trying to put the hose to me. It did not work. I told him again that he was not calling the shots and I would never say yes or no until I knew what the job was. I knew at this point that there was never a job and he and/or the Board could care less. Judah's plan was to treat me the same way he did Tom. Judah knew of my physical problems of being a diabetic and having a quad heart bypass eight years ago. He also knew that I had just paid off a $128,000.00 bill I knew nothing about until I finally received it. I had a few bucks left. I sold land and everything I could to pay off this debt and I did. So, he knew my financial situation at this point in my life so he thought I would take the position no matter what. He was wrong again because he never really knew me or cared. If I had not done my job I could understand. But, I knew I had done far beyond my job and my evaluations would prove it. I knew for a long time the Board had the wrong person as superintendent but he was the man in charge and there was nothing I could do about it. We were the same age and I knew Judah did not want to look for another job at our age and neither did I. My daughter was about to have her first baby and I wanted to be around to see its birth and help her out in anyway I could. I was not looking for another job at this point and had no reason for moving. I thought I had a lot of friends and I liked where I lived. I still believe it's a great place to raise a family. I never had to worry about my children and now I was waiting for my first grandchild. What could be better?

Judah thought I would just take the job no matter what it was because of my financial and physical conditions I had to live with. He didn't know I was willing to give up everything I had and then some for what I believed in. I did tell Judah what was going on in my life at the time I would most likely take the job if they would only meet with me and tell me what it was. But, they chose not to meet with me again. One Friday night I called Judah at home and asked him to set up a meeting for Monday morning to go over the job and we could put this issue to rest. He said he had to make a call first and then he would get back to me. I said fine. As I was waiting for his call I decided to call Joan to see if that was the person he had to talk to and her line was busy. I knew now who was actually running the show. I called her back a few minutes later and her line was open and I hung up before Joan answered her phone. I did not know if she had ID on her service but I said what the hell. What did I have to lose? Within two minutes Judah called me back and said the Board and he would meet with me on Monday morning at his office at 7:00 a.m.

When Monday morning came around I was there at 6:45 a.m. and I waited outside in my car for the rest of them to arrive. I waited and waited for nearly two hours when Judah finally showed up. We went to his office and he told me the Board would not meet with me and wanted the school's attorney at the meeting. I could not believe what I was hearing. It was going to take an attorney to work out a job description for this new position? I thought this was a dumb idea but the Board had now brought a third party into it, the school's attorney. I was in total shock. At this time I had to decide if I was going to fight fire with fire or still try to work things out. The

Board made their decision and now it was up to me. I knew what it meant to my job and career in education if I sued. I decided to try and work things out and wait for a meeting. I waited nearly four months and no meeting was ever called like I was promised. Something or someone was stopping the whole process and I knew who it was. From information I received from a Board member, it was not the Board. It was Judah. He wanted me out of the picture at any cost to the district. The Board member told me the Board wanted to settle the matter but Judah would not agree. So they drew the battle lines and for the first time a third party was involved.

I finally figured out after the Board decided not to pursue Judah and to go after me. I did not go through the ranks of a teacher and then an administrator in this district. At this point I was the only one who did not have something called tenure in the district. If the Board had gone after any other administrator in the district who was qualified that person could have bumped back into their teaching position. This would have bumped someone else out of their teaching job and they would have had a major problem on their hands. The Board wanted to make a change and it was either Judah and/or myself. I had only lived in the district for eighteen years and that wasn't enough time for a conservative district to accept someone. If I had come through the teaching ranks as all the rest of the administrators had with tenure as a teacher the Board would have had nobody to bring down. But, that wasn't the case with me and for that reason I became the target of their misery.

At this time I decided just to do my job and wait and see what develops. As the teachers told their students what had happened the students decided to take matters into their own hands. They started to organize against the actions of the Board and support me in whatever way they could. They formed a petition signed by almost the entire student body along with their parents' signatures. They organized a walk-out and invited Channel 5 to cover it. The juniors decided not to participate in taking the MEAP tests that would have meant a lost of $4,000.00 to every student who passed. If you times this times at least 100 students who passed the MEAP that would total an additional $400,000.00 they were willing to give up for my cause. One counselor was so worried about the juniors not taking the state's tests and the money the students and their families would lose he called the state and told them what was happening. The state said they never had a school refuse to participate in taking the MEAP tests and really didn't know what they would do if the students refused.

After hearing all the above I knew I had to do something. I could not allow the students and parents to lose this total amount of money for me. So I met the members of the Junior class and talked them out of their decision of not taking the state's tests. It was just too much to possibly lose in a low-income district like it was. But, this told me I was right about students in general. When they believe in a cause and they believed in me there was no limit for them to give up. I knew we had a great relationship but I never wanted to use the student body or have them lose so much. The walk out was another story. Along with the signed petitions the students made signs and posters and invited many former students back to participate. I never knew they were so well organized and supportive.

This became the greatest mistake I had ever made. On the morning of the planned walk out I thought the Board was still going to sit down with me and work out this new job they were talking about. I was also told this planned walkout was going to happen day after day until the student body won and I was going to their principal once again. The students knew my assistant principal and hated him and what he stood for. Mr. Wills really didn't care about them and they knew it. He was to busy running around on his wife after having three children with her and stabbing me in the back every chance he could. He let it be known he was going to take my place as principal next year and he would be in charge. This brought the student body out of the woodwork because they had his number. But, I did not ever want the student body to take it this far and talked them out of walking out for me. I could tell their disappointment just by looking at them but I thought their parents would be at the next Board meeting in mass and this whole thing would be over once and for all. I had received many calls from parents who told me they would be at the next Board meeting along with the student body and I had nothing to worry about. But, that never came about. The parents and the community let me down. To this day I know if I had allowed this planned walkout I would still have my job but I knew the district was planning on punishing them for their actions and I would never put them at risk. I guess I will never know what would have actually happened but things did not work out for me by taking the action that I did. It was my own fault and I only had myself to blame.

The rest of the school year went well and my relationship with the student body never changed. I was thinking about walking out at graduation but it was the students crowning achievement and it went as planned. If I would have walked out I know the seniors would have followed and received their diplomas at a later date. I knew this was their big event in their lives and I was not about to spoil it. So, I told the seniors it was not going to happen at graduation no matter what. They did what I asked them to do and graduation went off without a hitch.

A few months before graduation I walked by my assistant principal door and noticed him on the phone. I wondered whom he was talking to and waited for him to leave his office. I went in his office and found out whom he called and he was talking to. It was Joan Harmond. He knew I was on top of things so I asked him whom he called. He always told me he never called her but she would call him almost every day. This time I caught him in another lie because he called her. Now I knew there was nobody left I could trust in the district.

I had to call the placement office at Central Michigan University a few days later because I had a teacher who was not coming back and I needed her replaced. The placement office informed me Mr. Wills had called them to look for the same replacement and he was the high school principal and not myself. I still had a few months to go before school was out and he was jumping the gun. I did realize he was promised my job by Judah and Mrs. Joan Harmond long before this matter was finished. Some people seem to do anything to get ahead. In a way it worked out in my favor. I knew exactly where I stood and all I had to do was wait and see how things would now work out. I would not be surprised ever again. More than twenty years ago Mark's father was one of my coaches who worked for me at St. Stephens Area High School.

I wondered how his father now felt about his son? I do not believe his father would have done what his son was doing. I knew now Mark was a complete piece of shit.

On Friday, June 18, 2004 I received a call from Judah. He said he wanted me to report to Standish Elementary on Monday and to clear out my office. I called Roger at the elementary to see if he knew I was coming. He said he had not heard a word from Judah and I would have to take a vacant classroom and sit there by myself. Does this remind you of anyone?

I was ahead of the game and already had my stuff packed and ready to put into my car. I stopped by my doctor's office before going home. My doctor, Linda Runner was not in so I saw her medical assistant. She was aware of what I was going through and told me to take a few days off work to relax. I guess my blood pressure was sky high and my sugar was out of whack. So I went home to do what she prescribed. I had 135 sick days built up that was the highest a person could get at the time. On the next three days I called in to work sick with the doctor's excuse. On the third day I was told Judah had informed the Board I resigned and I would no longer be working for the district. This was a complete lie on his part. I could now see the writing on the wall and Judah left me no choice but to get a lawyer and sue the district for what they were doing. I knew a lawyer in Bay City I went to school with and decided to give him a call. He knew what I was calling about because Gloria and I had talked to him right after the Board told me they would not sit down with me and wanted their attorney involved but that never came about. I knew their move not only meant my job but also my career. I wondered how these people could ever look in the mirror without seeing the devil looking back at them. These types of people seem to live with themselves no matter what they do.

No letter was ever sent to Judah stating anything about resigning or anything of that sort. Judah made it up and the Board bought it. An all out war was about to take place that the Board caused along with Judah doing his dirty work. I never wanted to get lawyers involved and never wanted to sue the district to begin with. This was their choice and they now drew the lines.

Chapter XI

FIGHTING FIRE WITH FIRE

HIRING A LAWYER

I called my old attorney and found out he had retired and his son and daughter who I had in high school at St. Stephens were now running his office. I talked to his son and he must have been to busy and never gave me an answer. I then called the individual I had gone to school with and hired him. His name was Kim Biggs and it became one of the biggest mistakes I ever made. Gloria and I set up an appointment with him to go over my case and what was happening. Like I said before I never wanted to sue the school district but they left me no choice. Judah knew my health situation and knew I had to have blue-cross coverage just to pay my bills. When we first talked to Kim he said we should sue for around $2 million and that's what decided to go for. His fee was going to be around 1/3 of whatever we received so we signed a contract about a week later. Now, at least we had an attorney to talk with the other side. We were now fighting fire with fire. Kim went to the same high school I had gone to, Bay City Central. He graduated a year ahead of me. His father was a judge while his sister was also an attorney and judge. In school he was the student council president while I had only been a class representative.

Kim was a conservative politician and that scared me a little. By this I mean he was in practice to change very little. Knowing him and his family background I thought he would do a good job representing me in court. Like you will see I believe he was working for the other side most of the time and made so many mistakes I wanted to fire him many times over. But, I knew most attorneys were as corrupt as anyone and they were really out for what they could get for themselves.

I had a bad taste in my mouth with my association with my mother's attorney when I was fifteen years old and never trusted them from then on. My mother who was and is a saint in heaven hired an attorney when my father divorced my mother. I remember towards the end of her case her attorney asked her to get the divorce because it would look better in the paper and she did. She just wanted to get divorced at the time for her and her children's sake. My father was not a good person and when he left in was a heavy burden taken off our shoulders. For the first time in my life I felt somewhat at ease. I knew my mother and my two brothers and two sisters felt the same way. Anyways, around two months after their divorce my mother received a bill from both attorneys. Her own attorney never told her by finally getting the divorce she had to pay the bills. My father was aware of what was happening and actually took the money from his own children.

My older brother and I went looking for her attorney but he could not be found. I think if we would have found him something bad would have happened. Now, you know why I did not have any faith in ever hiring any attorney. After going through my case I swore I would represent myself before I would ever hire an attorney again. If you keep reading, I think you will see why. In my opinion being an attorney is only a license to steal. I have never known of one that actually worked hard for their pay. Real life attorneys are not like the ones on TV shows. I know there is a saying that only a fool represents himself or herself but I know I would stand a much better chance if the judge did not have to be an attorney himself or herself. I know it's our system but that doesn't make it right.

When the papers found out I was suing the school district both the local and Bay City Times contacted my attorney, Mr. Biggs. After speaking with him both articles came out stating I was suing for $500,000.00. I immediately called my attorney and asked him about the $2,000,000.00 figure we talked about. I had just lost 1.5 million dollars from what we decided starting out. Mr. Biggs really didn't give me an answer and took it upon himself to lower the figure. I should have fired him immediately but I didn't and went on from there. A hearing was set up in the 23rd. district in Standish, Michigan soon after Kim was hired of Judge Ron Bergermister to see if in his opinion I had a case or not. My attorney called me and gave me the date of this hearing and time. I told him I would be there early.

After we presented my case for the first time, the judge ruled I had a case and stated the school district should settle the case with me out of court. The district chose not to do this and things proceeded. I was waiting for the next meeting when Kim called me and asked where I was. I said what do you mean because I was starting to get a little worried. He told me the judge had another hearing yesterday and he ruled against me. I was really pissed off at my attorney because he never informed me about the second hearing. He said he thought he had but the damage was done. Someone had gotten to the local judge or he was playing politics with my life. I found out later both were true and now I was facing another dilemma. According to Kim we could either walk away at this point and forget about the whole thing or take it to the Appeals Court in the State of Michigan. Kim informed me this would mean a lot of work on his part and it would be new for him. He said the amount would now be a little more for his help and instead of 1/3 the amount for his services would increase by at least 10%. I had no choice in the matter because I was now out of a job for the first time in my life. I decided to take my case to the next higher level. Kim informed me it would take some time to get ready but he was going to do his job.

Right after I left the district I tried to get unemployment for the first time in my life but Judah denied me. He said it was my choice to leave but I think you know better. I was forced to do something without any income whatsoever. To receive my blue-cross/ blue shield coverage I had to retire and I did. It had nothing to do with my case and I needed the coverage. At the time I retired I had 18.5 years of credit in public education. A person needs at least ten years to qualify. Anything less than thirty years a person could receive a reduced rate but I needed the coverage.

Without any income I had to look around for a job. I thought this would be an easy task but I was wrong. People in the area would not hire me because I was now suing the local district. I applied at just about all the local establishments but was never hired. I had a few close friends who laughed at me and were no help. I started to apply and get my name out to college placement offices for either a teaching or administrative position. At this time I had to use my 401 K of about $40,000.00 I had built up for my retirement years that came much earlier than I ever expected. Because I retired early the government took an additional ten percent for retiring before I was sixty-two years young and penalized me. I was only 57 when I retired. So I did my best to stretch out what was left. In today's market and with the bills I had coming in my 401 K monies did not last long. I was now going broke and had to do something to survive. I did get hired at Roger McIntosh's car dealership in Linwood, Michigan to sell new and used cars. I thought for a moment this would be right up my ally because I was a good people person and I knew Chevrolets. When I started I went through a training period that usually last about three to four weeks. I had it completed in a few days and was looking forward to selling cars soon. It was a great place to work and the owner and I got along really well. I remember waiting on my first customer and had him ready to sign for a new Suburban if I could get the manager to give him a few more dollars for his trade in. But, the manager said no and the deal never materialized into a sale. The manager got a little upset with me when I told him what took him three months I did in a couple of days. I was even helping their salesmen pass their tests they were taking to remain a salesman for General Motors. The next time I went out to wait on a customer the owners' son-in- law told me to go out and see what that person wanted. So I did what I was told. I started walking towards new customer and the manager came out and told me to go back inside. I stayed thirteen days when I told the owner I could not work with their manager and decided to quit. The owner tried to talk me out of it but I also knew I felt guilty when I waited on a customer. Their salesmen were doing this for a living and they had young families to support. I was bored waiting for new customers who never walked in from the street. The dealership was located out in the country and people never just walked in. It seemed as though I was wasting my time. I knew from the beginning I was a different person than the ones working there. I was not the type to just sit around and wait for something to happen. I said my goodbyes and left. A few days later I was hired by a man in Bay City to become a landman. This was a person who leases land from the owners for so many dollars an acre. I truly liked this job and the pay was decent. I received $300.00 a day plus gas and food. The people I met were fantastic. I leased a lot of land and enjoyed the coffee and sweet things I was given. This lasted for a summer and the main company I was leasing for went belly-up. If I ever get the chance to do this again, I would do it in a minute.

The above two jobs were the only times I could find work but nobody hired me in the area I lived. The money I received for doing these two jobs helped my situation but did not last long. I was able to pay a few bills but my reserve was gone and I was living like a lot of people from check to check until Gloria and I became old enough to draw Social Security. So for a period of at least five years I really could not find employment.

A friend of mine in the last seven years Mr. Gary Osier gave me a job for one day. I painted one of his oil drums and did a good job. Gary has helped me out in different ways over the last seven years and I owe him and his son Todd for doing what they could. Aside from those two there was no one else. It sure taught me about true friendship and what that means. Everything has a limit and limit is usually the almighty dollar. If people think you are hurting for money they were never around.

Along with hiring Kim he talked me into paying $1,250.00 for the services of an accountant who determines what a person has and will lose in a case like mine. I figured it out myself and it came to around $450,000.00. The accountant came within a few dollars of what I expected. The sad thing about all this was my lawyer once again. Two years after I decided to sue and the first day of my case in court I found out Kim forgot to turn in my list of thirteen witnesses I had given him over two years before. The judge established deadlines for him to do this but my lawyer never did. The judge was also not going to allow the $1,250.00 accountant's report to be entered into the case. At this point I made an appointment with Kim. He was so screwed up I asked him if my case was too much for him to do. He said no but things never got any better. But at this point in my case it was too late to change lawyers. I should have never hired him in the first place and his blunders so far were proof of that.

While I was waiting for the Michigan Court of Appeals I was still looking for a job. I was interviewed for a principal position in many parts of the state. I was basically looking around where I lived to stay close to my daughter and now her two children. They became my first priority in life along with my wife, son and daughter. Their names are Madison Eustelle Moore and Nicholas James Moore. I believe they gave me a reason to keep going but never taking life so seriously again. I realized it's a big joke and I would never take it any other way. When I look at what's happening around the state, nation and the rest of the world it must be a joke-taking place on mankind. I just hope things get a little better because it can't get much worst for the majority of people in the world. If I were as serious as I use to be about what I see and know I would do whatever I could to change it. Now I am more like the rest of our human race and just let things slide and say there is nothing I can do about it. I believe this new attitude will give me a little more time on earth. I will live longer because there is no pressure. I'll just play the game I see as being stacked against us and let it go.

It seems as if I would get down to the last two individuals the boards were interested in hiring but I always ended up being number two. These school districts always ended up checking me out and giving a call to Judah. I can only imagine what he was saying. I know of one school district where I was asked about what I thought of loyalty. I told the board I thought it was a two way street. A person must be loyal in order for someone else to be loyal to him or her. If loyalty does not exit with the top dog the pack will never be loyal to its' leader. A person cannot treat his people like shit and expect true loyalty from them in return. It works both ways. After this interview I again ended up being number two and the job went to someone else. I realized the individual who asked me this question on loyalty was a veterinarian who worked with horses quite a bit. Judah and his wife had horses and I am sure they knew each other well. In fact he was most likely the vet who worked on Judah's horses for a few years. Most vets only see cat and dogs most of the time. Bigger animals are too hard to work with for the most part and so it goes.

The next interview I had was a job for the Superintendent of Augres Schools. I never brought up I was suing Standish-Sterling during my interviews until I went there. I had been told the job was mine if I wanted it so I decided to let them know what was happening with the suit. I explained things so well and in detail the Board thought I had a problem and chose another individual. Being a district just North of Standish-Sterling I figured they had a good idea as to what was happening but I wanted to get everything out in the open because I had nothing to hide. I ended up being number two once again. I finally gave up looking for an administrative position because Boards would not hire someone suing a school district no matter what the reason was. I did receive calls from three school districts in the upper peninsula of Michigan without ever applying. Two of the three offered me the position over the phone without ever talking to or seeing me. I told them I was not interested because it would take me to far away from my family and I did not want to live in that part of the state. After Augres I never applied again. It was my decision I could live with no matter what.

Chapter XII

THE INTERNET

SEARCHING THE WEB

After the Judge ruled against us at the circuit court level I was left appealing to the state court of appeals. This was a very depressing time in my life but I had to now take charge of my own case if the balance was ever going to switch in my favor. My lawyer was trying to prepare information for the court of appeals to look at and listen to the arguments presented. I told him to try and get the case in the courtroom of a non-bias judge so I could have a fair trial. The judge would not step aside for obvious reasons and Kim said he could not get the case moved. I still wonder if he tried to do this or not? I never saw anything stating he had.

This was when I took matters into my own hands and started searching the web for anything that would help my case along with my lawyer. All of a sudden I came across a law in the State of Michigan that fit my case to a tee. It was in the case law section of the laws within the state. It can be found on the Internet in the case of Sanders vs. Delton Kellogg Schools. This case was not exactly like mine but laws were established and all school districts must enforce. This case went all the way to the Supreme Court of the State of Michigan. I had my attorney base our case on the state laws established in this case while he was preparing his information for the Court of Appeals. I also knew right then and there if something positive was going to get done on my case it was now up to me to investigate the matter and inform my attorney. My attorney was not going to do it. We were into the second year on my case and until I found the law in my case I believe I was dead in the water. My attorney was not aware of the laws I found pertaining to my case and now saw a new tunnel of light on the horizon.

The next thing we had to do was to present my case to the court of appeals in Grand Rapids. This was a first time for Kim and myself going to this level and now we were looking forward to this challenge. Kim spent the night before we were scheduled to appear in court while Gloria and I drove down in the morning. I must say Kim's presentation was about as good as I could expect. The school district sent down an attorney from their office who was totally in the dark. I could not believe they could make that mistake. I do not believe their attorney knew anything and had nothing prepared. This was foolish on their part but I knew they still had the circuit court judge in their hip pocket. Their lawyers even told us they did. In my extra time I also read a book called "Darker Than Night" written by Tom Henderson. This book had nothing to do with my case but it told me more about the circuit court judge. The author, Tom Henderson states he has never seen a judge like him before. The judge actually never gave the attorneys for the two brothers a chance in his court. Again, the judge was totally bias in that case to. The judge would not let the defense attorneys say a word. The two brothers were guilty before they entered his courtroom. Both brothers were not given a fair trial from the beginning even though they were both found guilty in the end.

I knew we were still going to battle the judge again in the end because the State Court of Appeals did not take jurisdiction in my case. In other words their verdict meant nothing whatsoever. All we ended up getting was a verdict in our favor based on case law that actually meant nothing. The Appeals Court verdict can be found on the Internet in my case and it reads as follows:

CASE LAW FULL DISPLAY COURT OF APPEALS OF MICHIGAN MARCH 23, 2006, DECIDED NOTICE:

THIS IS AN UNPUBLISHED OPINION IN ACCORDANCE WITH MICHIGAN COURT OF APPEALS RULES; UNPUBLISHED OPINIONS ARE NOT PRECEDENTIALLY BINDING UNDER THE RULES OF STARE DECISIS.

SUBSEQUENT HISTORY: Appeal denied by Haut v. Standish-Sterling Community
School District.

PRIOR HISTORY: Arenac Circuit Court

DISPOSITION:

We reverse the circuit court's grant of summary disposition to defendants, and remand for proceedings consistent with this opinion. We do not retain jurisdiction.

JUDGES: Before: Bandstra, P.J., and White and Fort Hood, JJ.

OPINION

PER CURIAM.

In this action involving claims for breach of contract and violations of MCL 380.1229, plaintiff appeals as of right from the circuit court's order granting defendant's motion for summary disposition under MCR 2.116 © (10). We reverse.

This Court reviews de novo a circuit court's decision with regard to a motion for summary disposition. A motion under tests the factual support for a claim. In reviewing a motion under this Court "must consider the available pleadings, affidavits, depositions, and other documentary evidence in a light most favorable to the nonmoving party and determine whether the moving party was entitled to judgment as a matter of law." The Court "must consider the available pleadings, affidavits, depositions, and other documentary evidence in a light most favorable to the nonmoving party and determine whether the moving party was entitled to judgment as a matter of law"

Plaintiff alleges that defendants violated MCL 380.1229, which provides, in pertinent part.

The board of a school district or intermediate school district may employ assistant superintendents, principals, assistant principals, guidance directors and other administrators who do not assume tenure in that position under Act No. 4 of the Public Acts of the Extra Session of 1937, being sections 38.71 to 38.191 of the Michigan Compiled Laws. The employment shall be by written contract. The term of the employment contract shall be fixed by the board, not to exceed three years. The board shall prescribe the duties of a person described in this subsection is not given at least 60 days before the termination date of the contract, the contract is renewed for an additional 1-year period.

A notification of nonrenewal of contract of a person described in subsection (2) may be given only for a reason that is not arbitrary or capricious. The board shall not issue a notice of nonrenewal under this section unless the affected person has been provided with not less than 30 days' advance notice that the board is considering the nonrenewal together with a written statement of the reasons the board is considering the nonrenewal. After the issuance of the written statement, but before the nonrenewal statement is issued, The affected person shall be given the opportunity to meet with not less than a majority of the board to discuss the reasons stated in the written statement. The meeting shall be open to the public or a closed session, as the affected person elects under section 8 of the opens meetings act. If the board fails to provide for a meeting with the board, or if a court finds that the reason for nonrenewal is arbitrary or capricious, the affected person's contract is renewed for an additional for an addition 1-year period. This subsection does not apply to the nonrenewal of the contract of a superintendent of schools described in subsection (1). The purpose of this statute is to protect administrators from being arbitrarily removed from their administrative positions. Sanders v. Delton Kellogg Schools. By its express terms, the notice and meeting protections of the statute apply only to "nonrenewals" of a contract. As used in this statute, the term "nonrenewal" means either (1) termination from an administrative position, or (2) reassignment from an administrative position to a nonadministrative position. In this case, plaintiff claims that a nonrenewal within the meaning of S 1229 occurred. We conclude that a question of fact remained on this issue.

Viewed in a light most favorable to plaintiff, documentary evidence submitted below established that defendants never provided plaintiff with (*5) a written description of the alleged position-a position which had never existed before. Plaintiff was told to report to this "new position" in June of 2004, yet the position remained undefined and not formalized. Although plaintiff was told that he would receive the same salary and benefits that he received as a school principal, were he to accept this "position," this is not dispositive nor does it preclude the existence of a question of fact whether defendants' actions constituted reassigning plaintiff from an administrative to a nonadministrative position. We conclude that a question of fact remained on this issue.

We also agree with plaintiff that the current court improperly dismissed his breach of contract claim. The contract governing plaintiff's employment, entitles Standish-Sterling Community School District Administrator's Contract of Employment, stated in pertinent part:

1. Term of Employment. The Board of Education agrees to employ the Administrator in an administrative capacity for the term of (2) years from July1, 2003 to June 30, 2005.

    . . . Right to Reassign. The Administrator shall be subject to reassignment and/or transfer into

(*6) a new or different administrative .... At the sole discretion of the Superintendent in the event that the Administrator is reassigned to a different position, they (etc) will be provided, upon request, with a written statement of the reasons for the transfer ...

To the extent that plaintiff's breach of contract is based on his contention that he was reassigned to a nonadministrative position. It has been addressed above. Plaintiff also maintains that a viable breach of contract claim exists because defendants failed to provide him with a written statement of the reason for the reassignment, as required by the contract. The evidence established that defendants failed to provide plaintiff with a written statement of the reason for the reassignment, and plaintiff testified that he requested several times that defendants provide him with the reason(s).

We disagree with defendant's contention that plaintiff cannot maintain a breach of contract claim because plaintiff "outright refused to report to the administrative assignment and subsequently decided to voluntarily retire from any employment with

Standish." On June 11, 2004, plaintiff wrote Superintendent Foot.

The (*7) contract I signed with the Standish-Sterling School District was to be the high school principal. I have given the last eighteen years of my life to this district and have never been told or given any reason for this transfer in writing. With superior evaluations every year, I cannot find any reason for such a move. Therefore, I expect the board to honor my contract as principal of the school. (Emphasis added.) No written explanation was provided, but Superintendent Foot called plaintiff and instructed him to report to the alleged newly created position on June 21st. Plaintiff e-mailed Foot on February 15th. stating:

If you read my letter from last week, I believe it states I will not be taking this newly created position. Therefore, I will not be reporting to Standish Elementary this Monday,

June 21, 2004, as you indicated in your voice mail. I believe I have no other choice but to stay home and take my chance at a higher level. While Foot interpreted plaintiff's communication as a resignation, a reasonable fact-finder could conclude that plaintiff did not resign, but rather, chose to rest on the absence of a written explanation or job description and (*8) to pursue at a level higher than Foot and the Board. In fact, plaintiff filed this lawsuit on June 21, 2004.

We conclude that a genuine issue of fact remained whether plaintiff was reassigned from an administrative to a non-administrative position, and whether defendants breached plaintiff' contract.

We reverse the circuit court's grant of summary disposition to defendants, and remand for proceedings consistent with this opinion. We do not retain jurisdiction.

/s/ Richard A. Bandstra

/s/ Helene N. White

/s/ Karen M. Fort Hood

Chapter XIII

OUTCOME

SUPREME COURT & BACK TO BEGINNING

My case against Standish-Sterling Community Schools now went to the Michigan Supreme Court. The district had to take in there because they lost at the Appeals level. So the waiting game was on. The verdict came much faster than we planned. Sometimes I have been told it takes years. But in my case the Michigan Supreme Court decided in my favor once again. The Supreme Court actually went with exactly what the Appeals Court of the state said above.

I wondered what was going to happen next? I soon found out because the higher courts didn't hold jurisdiction in my case the trial went back to the Circuit Court in Standish, Michigan. I could not believe what was happening. We were starting over after all this time and money spent in a courtroom of a judge that in my opinion was totally incompetent. At this point I never knew he could do what he wanted without retribution. After you read the above I was pleased the courts took their time and investigated what exactly was taking place and decided the case based on the current laws governing cases like mine. I wondered how two higher-level courts could decide my case, take the action they did and then did not hold jurisdiction on the matter at hand. I eventually realized they wasted their time and money coming from the taxpayers of the state. If they were not going to hold jurisdiction in my case why didn't they just send it back and forget about the whole matter because I knew it was going nowhere back in the Circuit Court in Standish. The judge there had already played his hand and proved he was on the other side and nobody was ever going to change his mind. I know the higher courts instructed him to go by the law and to follow their recommendations but don't bet your life he would because you would lose. I now knew I was dead in the water and had nowhere to go but down the creek in a boat without a paddle.

But I was not giving up and the battle was about to begin once again in the Circuit Court. The judge's decision had been reversed and that really pissed him off. They could see the truth and knew the new administrative position was not an administrative position at all. They called it an alleged position because it never materialized. I was never given any reason for my transfer I had asked the board for many times. My resignation was a figment of Judah's imagination. My statement or e-mail to Judah on the 18th. of June was only a letter telling him I would be home waiting for his call to work out the description of the new job they cooked up in their minds but would not meet with me to go over the position because they made it up and there was no such thing. Judah wanted me to go down to Standish Elementary and just sit there like Tom did for a year. He was following the same scenario he put Tom through.

For a man who was the superintendent of schools he was not too bright. I can go on and on about what the courts agreed with me about and backed me on. The only thing I could do now was to sit around and wait. The major problem was Judah himself. This all could have been resolved with him and the school board if they would have only chosen to work with me. But, they refused because Judah thought I had a list of things on him my assistant principal made up in order to get my job as I have shown you already. It was like the system had a cancer spreading throughout the district and nothing was making any sense. I believe Judah's mind was melting away and caused him to be afraid for himself and his career. It was now impossible to work with him when he was going through this in his current mental state. I felt sorry for the district but especially for a man whom was once a friend turning into a coward and allowing the district to suffer and go down the tube. I knew the next individual following Judah would be in for one hell of a mess. He or she would never have a chance no matter who this person was and it was not going to be me. I was done with the district forever no matter what.

The next thing I found out while I was waiting to see what was coming next was another huge mistake by my attorney. Kim had dropped the age discrimination part of my lawsuit when I told him not to. This was a big item we had won without us doing anything. I was 57 years old at the time while my replacement was only 39 years young. His actual qualifications were a lot less than mine and the matter was in the bag. I could not believe what he had done. In fact I told him not to do it but he did anyway. I should have fired him on the spot but it was getting so late in the game I had to stick with him but I knew better. Kim was actually more concerned about getting some money than working for me. His actions were telling me he was actually working for the other side and I knew I could have another lawsuit coming down the pike.

I though what the heck could happen next? It wasn't long and Kim screwed me again but this time he did not tell me what he had done until just a few days before the trial started for the first time in the circuit court. The first time was when Judge Ron went in my favor and later changed his mind and said I did not have a case and was hoping it would die an early death. Two years before this I had given my lawyer a list of 13 people I wanted to call as witnesses for me at the trial. I assumed he had taken care of this matter and we were ready for anything the other side could make-up. I thought I had everything covered and the truth would finally come out.

I was wrong once again! My lawyer finally admitted to me he did not turn in the names of my 13 witnesses over two years before and Judge Ron along with the accountant I paid was not going to allow them into the case. The timeline had passed over two years ago. Surprise! Surprise! But my lawyer did serve the papers to appear in court to the opposition (Judah and the Board members). What would you think? Kim had not done his job and now he was actually bringing eight people to the court against me. I was the only witness I had and everything I planned went down the drain without my knowledge. I trusted my attorney and now I stood alone to win the war. Things were not looking good but at this point in the game I had no other choice but go it alone. I believe on the second day of my trial my lawyer got a call on his cell phone from his secretary back in Bay City. Gloria and I were so close to him we heard every word. His secretary told that he again forgot to turn in his list of witnesses to the court on time and today was the last day he could do it. He told her to take time out of her schedule and get the list to court before it was to late. I thought to myself that Kim overlooks the thing he must do quite a bit. I lost thirteen witnesses myself because of another one of his blunders.

On the morning of the first day of my trial Judge Ron Bergermister decided to pick the jury. He stated there would be seven jurors chosen to sit as a jury with one alternate. Each side asked the potential jurors about their background and if they knew anything about the case and/or if they had any ties to either party. A couple of the potential jurors were students of mine who had graduated a few years before. The other side chose not to have them on the jury and they were dismissed from the case. One lady was a co-worker of Judah's wife at West Branch-Ogemaw Heights. I told Kim to have her dismissed but the Judge said she could stay and be a juror. I just about walked out of the court at this point but held my cool. I knew things in court were not going to work in my favor but this was crazy and not right. So, I knew going in I had one vote against me along with the judge. Things were going to be hard to say the least.

After the jury was selected the court took a break and then the trial was to begin. During the break Kim once again had another surprise for me. After Kim, the accountant, and I agreed to the amount of around $500,000.00 I would be suing for, Kim decided to break this amount into two parts. This was never brought to my attention until this moment. I asked him just what the hell was he doing? Kim had asked me to go out and buy sheets of large paper and put all of my financial losses on it so we could use it in court. So I did this and had it done for nothing. Kim knew I knew the figures in my head better than he did and decided to take them off the cuff without the jury seeing anything whatsoever. I knew again he was going to play this by ear and he had not prepared one thing for my case and that's the way it turned out. I tried to meet with Kim many times before this day and we met only two times. The number of times we met never mattered because he never had anything and/or strategy for his presentation in court. He said he knew what he was doing but I knew better. He had nothing and just wanted the case over so he could be paid.

The way things went from this point on was not too hard to figure out. Kim took my salary for two years and benefits and came up with $206,000.00. This was from my contract the school district broke. The remainder went into the laws established by the State's Supreme Court in the case of Sanders v. Delton Kellogg Schools. This was the part of my case the judge ignored from the very beginning. I was hoping the letter from the Appeals and Supreme Courts would change the judge's mind but I knew it would end up having a negative effect on my case because it just got the judge pissed off being overruled. The amount for $206,000.00 was an amount we never came up with before. The salary amount plus benefits came to $125,000.00 a year. This was now a totally new figure Kim made up and presented to the jury. I could not believe what he put together without going over the figures with me before the trial. I was in shock and wanted to take a break as soon as I heard the new amounts. This was not the amount the accountant and I came up with while Kim just sat there and said nothing either in support or contrary to the package we put together. Before we actually got started the opposition asked if we would take a part of my lawsuit away. This was the part against Judah for not doing his job that would take him off the hook financially. I told Kim not to do it but he agreed with the other side. He thought it would clear things up in the juror's minds and work in our favor. In my mind it was another big mistake made by my attorney. The lawsuit was against Judah and the Board and not just the Board. To the jury it was telling them we did not have our shit together and we would be in for a long four-day trial.

I was the first person to take the stand and at this point had no idea where my lawyer was coming from. Kim just sort of rubbed it off by saying I knew the figures so well I could bring them up as we went along. This told me just that. His plan was he was hoping for the other side to offer a deal that never came about. The other side told him the Board wanted to settle the matter out of court but Judah (who never lost a case in court) wanted to run the show and refused. Like I have stated before Kim never had a plan in the first place and would be playing my case by ear. It was obvious Kim just wanted to seal a deal and get his money and run. The other side did offer a total of $10,000.00 to settle the case. I refused and told their attorneys they had to be joking. Kim even agreed with me because the amount was way to low to even think about and he would not be making the money he wanted.

After raising my right hand and taking the oath the trial began. Kim had nothing to present to the jury on paper and the report I had done did not match his new figures. As we started it became very obvious Kim was totally unprepared. The judge told him to keep his questions to me simple and I could answer them with only a yes or no. The judge did not want to hear what I had to say on anything. So I had to keep my answers as short as possible. I few times a comment made by myself would have explained my answers better for the jury but the judge stopped me many times to just giving a yes or no answer. I was at the point of walking out but I knew it would only hurt my chances and play into the judge's hand. Another thing we were told by the other attorneys was the judge thought my case was only worth about $70,000.00 and he would fill envelopes for the amount of money I was paid. This told me the judge had been talking to someone who changed his mind about my lawsuit. It was obvious. Corruption had now entered my case in the name of the crooked judge. But, he had just begun to play his cards and a lot more was coming down the pike.

Our original plan was to have Kim go through my evaluations for the eighteen years I had worked in the district. This would show the jury just how good a principal I was and Judah himself signed them all. Kim ended up skipping this whole part of my case because the other side agreed that I had been a superior principal and that was that. These yearly evaluations on my job performance could now be used for toilet paper. They were not worth the paper they were written on and meant nothing to anyone in the courtroom. I wanted Kim to make something of them but he didn't and he proceeded with the case. Kim then brought in the laws that the Superintendent and Board broke in my case. As soon as he started on the state laws the judge stopped the court proceedings and called in meeting in his chambers for the attorneys from both sides. This went on for days and every time the state laws were brought up a meeting in his chambers took place. Judge Bergermister was ignoring what the higher courts told him to do and there was nothing we could do about it in his courtroom. This kept happening about every ten minutes and we were going nowhere. Finally the Judge called for yet another meeting in his chambers and according to Kim the judge threatened him with a huge fine if Kim said anything at all about the laws. Most of what was in the laws was also in my contract with the school except the procedural items the board overlooked over two and a half years ago.

The judge said he would call for a mistrial if we tried to bring the law into the case. I told Kim to ignore the judge and get the case thrown out but he refused. I told him the board and the superintendent broke my contract and the state laws and whatever the fine was we would get the money back before the case was all over. But Kim refused and we moved on without bringing up the state laws ever again. Kim said he would bring the laws into the case again during his summation but he didn't. Now the major financial part of my case was history and we only had my contract with the district we could talk about. I knew I was now going to see very little if things kept going the way they had. I figured at least in a mistrial I could start again with a different lawyer and hopefully a different judge. Kim knew by now I wanted to fire him and with the fine the judge was going to lay upon him he made sure he didn't mention the state law again. I finished my portion of the case and for my side we only had the superintendent and board members to question. The rest Kim lost as I explained.

CHAPTER XIV

THE BOARD

MY WITNESSES?

With only the other side to question we called on Judah first. After giving the court his background Kim started questioning him about why anyone would get rid of his best administrator in the district? Kim explained I had the best evaluations, and was always put in charge of the district when he was gone for the day and/or weeks at a time. Judah knew I had never resigned but that wasn't what he told the board. He told them I had. Kim brought this to his attention and Judah stated I retired and it really didn't matter now. This was his way of covering his lie from the beginning. Kim then asked him if he had ever told the board I wanted a meeting to go over the new job. He said he was to busy the last four months of the year and forgot. He was busy all right working on his personal finances and making sure his losses were as little as possible. This was the time when people were losing money in the stock market on a daily basis.

Kim asked all the members of the board and they all said the same thing. They said they never heard about a meeting with Judah and myself. Judah told them I resigned and then retired from my position and was not interested in the new job. I could not believe what he was saying. He was admitting he did not do his job and he acted like he did not care. The only board member who was there at the time was Joan Harmond and she was not about to say anything to the rest of the board about it. She and Judah had this whole thing worked out a long time ago when the board never showed up for the meeting scheduled for that Monday morning. Joan knew about the meeting because she and Judah scheduled it with me but totally ignored coming. Joan always lies but at least we were getting some half-truths out of Judah. I thought the case should have ended right there. Judah screwed the whole thing up and he finally admitted it in court. Judah never finished his testimony on day one and was the first one we would talk to the next morning. Before we left for the day I looked into the eyes of the district lawyers and they were even shocked as to what he said. I had a feeling the next morning would be a little different and it was.

The next day came soon enough. The echoes were about to rush in again as each board member took the stand. Judah was the first to take the stand and Kim asked him about the statement Dave made to me at the first meeting two years ago. Kim asked Judah if Dave ever stated thirty-two years was long enough to be a high school principal. This was going to prove our age discrimination case was part of the lawsuit until Kim took it out without my permission. Judah ended up lying and responding in the same words as Joan and Virginia. He said he could not recall and we could see right away the lawyers had gotten to Judah and he was not going to tell the truth today. So we ended our questions for Judah a few minutes after he took the stand the next day.

Joan Harmond was next. I had warned Kim Joan was the type of person who will kill you with kindness but she is smart enough to stab you in the back at the same time. That was the way she started on the stand. She stated she never wanted to hurt me but she wanted a change in the system and I was the one the board committee chose. Boy, was that stretching the truth a bit as I have pointed out many times before. The surprising thing was the judge allowed her to comment on whatever she said. This was something he told me I could not do. All this can be found in the court transcripts located in the Arenac County Courthouse located in Standish, Michigan. This is public information made available to anyone who wants to take a look. It was hard enough sitting through the trial let alone seeing and hearing these board members lying at will. The truth of the matter was Joan and I never liked each other one bit. I believe I have proven this many times so far in this book. She will never be free and someday die from her miserable life. Remember, only the truth will set you free and if this is so she has a hell of a lot of truth to get out before she meets her maker. I wish her the best but I have my doubts according to the life she lived. She only has to remember the wife of the doctor she ran with for years. She was certainly no educational leader for our children unless they wanted to live a life of sin and misery. She ended up saying she did not recall to just about everything Kim asked her so we moved on.

Virginia Bucowski was our next witness but we had to tape her answers for the jury because she was just to busy to go to court because of her job. She was a nurse and she was needed at work like the rest of the board members. I did not want to do it but in the end we had no choice if we wanted her answers and we did. Contact was made with the ISD out of Bay City and they agreed to tape our discussion with Virginia a few days before the trial began. Virginia was put on the board because she was a childhood friend of Joan Harmond. Her only purpose was to help Joan get what she wanted at any cost. She never knew what she was suppose to do as a board member and did not care. In her taped conversation she said some off the wall things. She was not being informed on matters involved in my case and for that matter she had no idea what the schools were all about. She wanted to get off the board and the sooner the better. She stated if I did not want this new position I would still be the high school principal. I wish the two other members of the board committee thought the same and none of this would have ever taken place. She did respond with the same comment, as I am sure their attorneys instructed them to. I don't recall was said by her about as many times as Joan. I believe her comments would have helped my case. But someone screwed up in court because they could not get the equipment to work and the tape was never showed to the jury. Her comments showed me many things I already knew. The board committee had no idea of what they were doing and really didn't care. The committee itself was split on not only the alleged new position and what they intended for me. Like I have stated before the committee should have presented me with what this new position was all about from the very beginning. Things would have gone a lot smoother for them and myself included. But, this was not the case and we both ended up spending a lot of time and money on something that should have never come about in the first place. This is what you get when you jump the gun and put matters into the hands of three people speaking for the entire board without being held responsible for their actions. This whole matter was never brought out at a single board meeting like it should have been and voted upon. The board and the public could care less. Judah was at least right about what he said some two and a half years before. He said people really do not care and this is the society we live in. I did not believe this then but I do now. The fact of the matter is simple. My job and my career were taken away for no reason whatsoever. At least the board never gave me one. I asked many times for a reason and I was never given one and we ended up where we are. My whole career came to an end because of three incompetent people who didn't care about me, the students and the district in general.

Dave Sondberg was the next to take the stand. He was the gentleman who at the time owned the restaurant I went to in Sterling every weekend. He was the one who made the comment about me being a high school principal for thirty-two years and he thought it was enough. Remember every board member and Judah who had taken the stand stated they could not recall if Dave made the comment for the board. It was his restaurant the majority of board members met illegally to plan their strategy of how to get rid of Judah and myself at any cost. I remember in Virginia's comments she stated she goes to this restaurant all the time. She was there with the committee but in the twenty- five years I have been going she has never been in this restaurant before or after. I know the committee and at least two other members were there because my friends told me. They would swear to it in court if I wanted them to. But when Kim did not turn in my list of thirteen witnesses it became meaningless.

If you remember Kim and I disagreed on the age discrimination part of my lawsuit he took out even after I told him not to. He was right so far because the board and Judah could not recall what he had said at the time. To Kim's surprise Dave finally admitted saying what I said he had said. Kim never thought he would ever admit to saying it but he did on the stand. Our age discrimination part of my original lawsuit was now proven. It also pointed out Judah and the board members lied on the stand. I believe it's called perjury in a real court of law. But Kim chose not to pursue the matter any further. I told him to call everyone who committed perjury back on the stand to see if they would now remember but he would not. It was just another indication he was working for a settlement and not looking out for my best interest.

Dave actually did not care at all about the school district like I stated before. He was thinking about moving back to the Detroit area he was from until he was elected to serve on the board by Joan and her followers. He lost the restaurant shortly thereafter and ran again for the board. This time I got the word out and he came in last out of six candidates running. The first time he received more votes than anyone. Now the people knew better. Thank God!

Dr. Ron Shob was the one who blamed me for his son, Jeff, not reaching his potential. My bottom line with this obsessed individual was he never bothered to come in and tell me what his son was doing. I had sent him to one of the high school counselors and never heard from him again until he got on the board by receiving 21 votes. But, like most people he had to blame someone and I became person in his warped mind. On the stand he admitted he and I didn't care for each other. He never told the entire truth by telling the jury he and Joan were the two responsible for getting me out in the first place. In my opinion by not telling the whole truth he ended up lying and not standing up like a man.

Jack Snowfield was supposed to be next but he was never served with the papers before the trial began. His friend was Ron and he served on the board to do whatever Ron told him. I was hoping to get Jack on the stand because he was a follower of Christ and would hopefully tell the whole truth. He might have become the one board member who did. But, that never came about. But someday the one and only real judge will evaluate his performance on earth. I think he will be in a lot of trouble in the hereafter wherever he ends up going.

Dr. Lenny Lubare was next to take the stand. This is a man I supported and voted in on the board many times. I believe he has now served on the board longer than anyone else. He is a popular individual within the community and Judah did not do anything without first checking with him. Now I know him and what's he about, I believe he should get off the board immediately if not sooner. He took the stand and stated he was left in the dark on my whole situation. He told me there was nothing he could do about what was happening. When he took the stand and stated he was left in the dark on everything, I knew right then he was lying because of what he told me before the trial began. Here was a man I supported for years covering his ass and letting me go down the drain. He was supposed to be a friend but like Judah he only cared about himself. I always considered his wife and oldest daughter special people who cared about others but I was wrong. They could not stand up to Dr. Lubare and he knew it. I have always felt very sorry for him and his family from the day he took the stand. At least he had his business blacktopped by the school for nothing. With him now out of the way only one board member was left.

Penny Sage was the last to take the stand. She had been on the board my entire 18 years I had been the high school principal. She was known as a Judah supporter for years. She actually knew everything happening in the district for years. She was now raising four daughters by herself because her husband was one of those individuals like my father. Her husband was a medical doctor who had been fooling around on her for many years and I could only feel her pain. Her best friend had been having an affair with her husband but she was like my mother and would not believe all the rumors going around the community. One day she came into my office but her mind was made up and she would not listen to what I knew about her husband's little affairs.

The mother of her best friend told me everything about what was going on with her daughter. She even told me who made the first move at a conference in Las Vegas. Betty Snodgrass was one of my best friends who passed on before the trial began. She was going to be one of my thirteen witnesses but you know what happened to that. I know Betty would have been there for me unless she was dead and that's what happened. I always believed Penny and her four daughters. I could feel their pain because I have in a way lived her life and saw what this type of thing can do to a mother and her children. For this reason alone I never had her husband treat me even though he wrote me a great recommendation when I was looking for another job. I never asked him for one but he had done it as a friend and supporter. He even offered me a job working for him checking urine on prisoners around the state. I declined the offer because I was not the type of person he needed.

Penny was the only board member I trusted at the time. She asked me before the trial if I really wanted my job as principal of the high school. I told her if Judah was still going to be my boss I would have to decline the offer. She said the committee was not in charge of anything because it takes the entire board to do what they wanted and no discussion has yet taken place. In fact the board as a whole never discussed the issue whatsoever. It was never put on the agenda and no discussion ever took place on my position and/or the alleged new job. Penny said to her knowledge there was never going to be a new position and I believed her. She was the only board member who cared and/or talked to me after I left. I tried talking to Lenny but he said he should not be talking to me and left it at that.

As a whole the entire board except Penny lied on the stand. I never heard so many "I don't recall" in my life. They were well coached by their attorneys and if I did not know any better I would have believed them. Their attorneys had their shit together for my trial. They had many posters to explain what they were saying to the jury and used an overhead to put a picture in the jury's mind. I was impressed with what they had done and I wanted my lawyer to do the same. Walking into court on the first day I thought we were going to do likewise but Kim screwed me once again. Kim had absolutely nothing ready except what I did and he did not use my charts anyway. As my lawyer he ended up costing me just about everything in the end. Needless to say, I would never hire him again. Maybe he should be stuffing envelopes with the judge?

One thing the other side tried to do was say I said I would take the new position and later changed my mind. Of course this was all a lie. I could not believe they were now trying to do anything to win this case and it would have worked if I had not been there. My lawyer let it go until I told him to put me on the stand again. I had looked in the summary of my deposition and found the quote. They forgot to finish my statement and left it out of what I had really said. Kim put me back on the stand and I finished the part of the quote for the jury. I said I would take the job once I met with the board and all agreed what this new job was all about. This never happened because there was no new administrative position and the board was not going to meet with me to work a description out. I knew Judah did not want the board involved in working on a job description and he and Joan made sure it would never take place. Judah had no choice but to play according to Joan's rules if he wanted to save himself and he did.

Judge Ron Bergermister was without a doubt the worst judge I have ever known. In high school he was a little weasel and was picked on most of his life. In my case the other side bought him. The state laws he had been elected to enforce didn't matter as he chose to ignore them completely in my case. By him not allowing my attorney (Kim) to say one word about what the law stated the jury had no idea as to what it said. The judge knew what he was doing and he did not care in the least.

Every time the trial broke for a few minutes he ran to his house across the street. I did not have to wonder what he was doing because his reputation preceded him. He has a major problem with alcohol and I knew what he was doing. Many days I wanted to call in the sheriff and have him tested but that would never happen. I still see him quite a bit at the local casino and he almost always has a drink in his hands the entire evening. A few times I wondered how he could drive home but in Arenac County the local authorities would never issue him a ticket anyways. It comes down to whom you are like in most other communities. Life is just not fair with this type of people running the show.

His actions in his court remind me of the show "Judge Judy". I do not believe she should be on for the public to watch. She like Judge Ron will never allow someone to talk if she does not agree with what is about to be said. They are about as rude as anyone can be and to a point think they're God in their courtroom. In the case of Judge Ron there should be some form of check and balance system built into our system. When I started my trial just about everyone who worked in the courthouse and knew him better told me what a terrible judge he was and to be careful not to piss him off. He seems to be very opinionated in most of his cases and does not try to hide it. Personally, I believe he is not smart enough to hide his emotions if he wanted to. In all honesty he should have taken himself out as the judge in my case to begin with. He knew everyone involved in the case and many of them were his personal friends he favored in court. I believe this can be seen in the transcripts of the case. But, like in my case when he thought he was God without any accountability to anyone. The voters screwed up when they voted him in and he has screwed up ever since. I often wonder how a man like him could ever pass the bar exam? The last time the voters voted him in was because his opponent did not file his papers properly and Ron actually won before the voters cast their ballots. If this is the type of lawyers and judges we have representing us in court I never want to be part of this system again. This is another reason why I haven't taken my lawyer to trial.

The judicial system in our country needs a lot of changing from what happens now. I actually wasted over two years of my life playing the brotherhood game as I call it in winning my case. Yes, you heard me right. Except for the one voter on the jury the rest voted in my favor in finding the school district breaking my contract. The jury awarded me a grand total of $103,000.00 and my lawyer took just about half. I could not do anything because the court sends the money to the attorney even though in my case Kim did not deserve one penny. He covered himself first and foremost. The district felt so bad for me they finally offered me $130.000.00 to settle. Kim told me to take the money or we would have to begin again. I wanted to tell them to kiss my ass but the bills were coming in faster than I could pay them off with no income and/or job I had no other choice.

When Gloria and I walked out of the courthouse on the fourth day of my trial I was not a happy camper. Because the jury went in my favor Kim was as happy as could be. He was now going to get paid even though his actions cost me over $400,000.00 he was getting a check. As we were walking to my car, three of the jurors came up to us and asked us if we were happy because they thought I had my job back and the district and judge really screwed me in the first place. I told the three ladies they did not understand what they had just done. I told them I did not have my job back because they had to find in my favor on the state laws the district and the judge ignored and I did not receive a penny for this part of the case. They told us they thought I would get my job back along with the money and things would be back to the way they should be. But, they were mistaken. One lady said they were going to go back in and see the judge about what just happened and I wished her the best as we drove away. I never heard from this group again but I knew the judge would never reopen the case again. So, I won and lost at the same time. I thought if Kim would not have broken the case into two parts like he did the day the trial started without telling me what he was going to do and/or getting my permission I might have received my job as principal back along with a lot more money to pay my bills. After the case was over I was still in the red so to speak and had nowhere to turn for help. I called the State of Appeals Court and told them what the judge had done but there was nothing they could do. If you remember they did not hold jurisdiction in my case and their hands were tied.

If I had to do it over again knowing everything I now know and how things went, I would have still gone to court with me being my own attorney. I know I would have done a better job than Kim had done and would have won and saved a lot of time and money.

I would like to say my story ends now but once an educator always an educator. I will do whatever I can to help someone in need for the rest of my life. My days are successful if I have helped someone out on any given day. I believe this is God's plan for me and now he has given me the time to do what he wanted me to do with the remainder of my time on his planet Earth. I know I will never have any extra cash but I will be fine. Right now I am working with a couple, as a parent advocate trying to get some needed help for their blind son. The Standish-Sterling School District says they are doing all they can but the case will end up in mediation and going to a higher-level if the district does not test the young man to find out his abilities and needs. This young man has to feel his worth to be successful in his life. The district has signs in the halls of the school bragging about them putting the students first and foremost. How about helping this boy reach his potential? They seem to talk the talk but never will walk the walk.

Before my story ends, the conclusion must be read. After my case was done and I was done with the district the board members who cost me my job and career seemed to disappear from the board except one as I have explained earlier. Jack resigned from the board before his term was done. Virginia never ran again while Joan and Ron resigned from the board and Dave was beaten to the floor the last time he tried to get elected again. As a group they had done their dirty work and chose to leave the board and not work for God's children because like I have said throughout this book they really didn't care about anyone else except themselves. I still believe their day is still coming either on Earth or in the next world. Do I forgive them for what they did? No, I never will. There is only one that can actually forgive them but I wish them the best of luck in trying to be forgiven by the one who knows. I look forward to judgment day. I do plan on seeing my mother and being with her when I go.

I will leave you with one final thought about my attorney before I come to my final conclusions. I picked up the local paper out of Bay City one day about six months after my case was finished and I noticed an article about my attorney Kim. He was just given an award for being the attorney of the year in Bay County. If this is not the Peter Principle at work in our society, I can't imagine him receiving anything but a swift kick you know where. Winning my case most likely had something to do with it. I thought if they only knew the number of great errors he made in my case alone. This just goes to prove what this country has come to. If he is the best in Bay County at any given time, I can only imagine what the other lawyers are like. But, I still have hope for this profession. If you ever find one like the programs on television, please send me his name and address and I will check him or her out.

CHAPTER XV

BITS AND PIECES

ST. STEPHEN'S AREA HIGH SCHOOL
BAY CITY ALL SAINTS HIGH SCHOOL
STANDISH-STERLING CENTRAL HIGH SCHOOL

The three schools I spent my career at were actually all great schools when it came to the students attending. My story so far has depicted things I remember happening at each educational institution. Each one had its' good and bad points but I would like to finish my story by only looking at the good points of each and not dwell on the negative. This would mean I will only write about what kept me at each school.

I will begin with St. Stephen's Area High school and the students who actually made up the school. The students were the best I could ever imagine. Sure there were times I wondered about a few of them but as a body they made my fourteen years there a pure pleasure and joy to serve. I was only twenty-three years old when I started teaching there. The seniors were mostly eighteen and I could not have started my career under better circumstances. As a group they came from well-to-do families and their talent and abilities could stack up against any other educational institution in the State of Michigan. When it came to any kind of testing such as the MEAP and/or ACT they were far above the average. If they had a fault it was most of them knew it. But, they were a joy to work and be with. No matter what happened they took their bumps and pleasures with a positive and mature attitude only they could do. If you remember the infamous ski trip, sixty-three students were suspended and knew what they had done, and took the punishment without a complaint. I had a much harder time with their parents but never with their children. Students actually know the difference between right and wrong. They would always admit when they screwed up and take the punishment handed out.

As a school, St. Stephens' was a great place to work I knew I would never get rich doing what I chose to do as a profession so the money never entered my mind while I worked there. At one point I never thought I would leave this school. I must admit I could have signed up for welfare while I was working but that never came into my mind. The families and friends I made there will never leave my mind and soul. It was a place I was always proud of working at but I knew deep in my mind I could never find another school like it anywhere. If I had to rank them compared to the other two high schools I would have them on top in most categories.

I always wanted to compare our scores with the public schools but that was not allowed back then. Now the public schools are compared to each other on the state MEAP tests and are ranked against each other just like the students. I must admit I believe this is a major mistake by our National and State Public institutions. There is nothing wrong with the state "Yes" and National "No Child Left Behind" programs except they will never reach the outcomes educators want. Believe it or not, there are still families in this country that have never had a child graduate from high school let alone college. How do you think these students perform on the MEAP tests each and every year? I think you know. The government has all the statistics needed to really make some positive changes in our system of education. As things work out only about twenty percent of our graduating classes each year go on for further studies after high school. Of that number only around 50% of these students ever graduate from college. With all the stats backing up what I am saying and all the money and time being spent, something is not working.

I believe a better way would be to take all the BS out of what's going on and first work with what we know. We know a person's IQ is established at an early age in life. It really does not change much if any, as the individual gets older. You can't get blood from a rock. So, it's time to look into a better way of educating students so they have some self-respect and just maybe get a job. Wouldn't this be better than maybe graduating from high school and never getting a decent job so a person can support a family instead of living off the government for the rest of their life? We now seem to be a society of non-workers. The incentives are just not out there. People have lost their self-respect and are going nowhere. The college graduates have a much better chance but can't seem to find work in their field and in the end join the lines for more government handouts.

I believe a better way to reach our students would be to test them as soon as possible and find out what students will be able to do with what they have. This is done in many European countries and a lot of the waste I see in this country is no longer there. Testing students each and every year on matters they don't care about is a waste of time. I have watched students for many years take the MEAP and ACT test because they have to. Many students never try because they do not plan on attending institutions for higher learning. This is what it's all about. How many college graduates are not working?

In England the test is called the 11plus exam and it measures a student's ability and interest levels. It is not given each and every year of a student's life. Students can then be placed either in college courses or trained for jobs going to be in great demand in the future. Students will be allowed to take the test a second time but that's it. If a student does not show he or she does not have the ability to succeed in college why should we waste the time and effort needed? These students can start their training while in high school for a career. Junior Colleges seem to be better prepared for what needs to be done than the institutions of higher learning like Michigan and Michigan State Universities.

High schools will actually need two different forms of curriculums. One for the college prep and one for the vast majority of students in some type of vocational training for a job and a life after high school. Schools such as our high schools, vocational technology schools at Career Centers and Junior Colleges around the nation are mostly set-up to handle whatever we need to make this work. Students will then graduate from high school with the skills they will need while preparing for the future. Now, only 10% actually finish programs that can get these students a job and find employment. We have forgotten about the 90% not trained in anything. The time is right to make the changes we will need. The time and money we will save is astronomical. We will no longer be a system of non-producers and more people will be content and happy in their lives. Self-respect and the belief in America along with caring just might come back. We seem to be going nowhere with our present educational system. College is just not for everyone.

All I seem to read about is we are falling behind other countries each and every day. The Japanese and Chinese students seem to out perform our students in just about every category tested and this is all BS. In those countries and many others the students are tested and then tracked in fields of training and studies long before they finish high school. They take their top students and only test and compare them with 100% of our students. No wonder why the results are the way they are. We should only be testing our top students and comparing them with these students from other countries. In the end who actually cares anyway? As long as we are meeting our needs and the needs of our students what more can you ask for? If we are comparing our students with the best in other nations let's start by comparing apples with apples. Our system reminds me of a fruit salad going nowhere except down our stomachs. As of today we are not a productive nation producing anything that matters. We have what it takes to make the changes will need for the future. Let's give it a chance to work in the right direction and once again lead the world into the future we want and need.

The three schools I have had the pleasure of working with all seem to be trying to make the changes they will need to be something they can be proud of. Sure they have problems to work out but they have started to head in the right direction. But, they will not be able to do it alone. Our future lies in our children. We should be doing everything we can to help them along the way. Instead of getting in the way of what's needed our society should be supporting change for the next generation. Things have not worked in the past will never work in the future. Holding on to an educational system not meeting the needs of the future is a waste of time and money. Why should we spend our money on something not working to begin with?

I have taught and watched students totally bored in and with school. A lot of this happens because the smarter students are so far ahead of the average students they just about put themselves to sleep in the classroom. When a teacher's lesson plan is geared towards the middle of the road students the two extremes are lost. The lower academic students are lost because things are much harder for them while the other extreme, the gifted students know most of what the teacher is covering already. I know this is the time to individualize the teacher's instructions so everyone gains something from each lesson. This is exactly what we pay our teachers to do. But, let's be honest. Most teachers have little time and lack the knowledge to completely challenge each student. This would be neat but we would need a few more teachers and/or aids to do what's needed. With the present budget situations in Michigan and around the country this would make it economically impossible. I believe if the students were tracked based on their IQ and interest levels it would meet more of what the students need. We have to forget what has been done in the past educationally. It has not worked for the most part. The time is right to make the changes we will need to meet the new demands we have put upon ourselves. It might cost the country a few more dollars in the beginning but the profits will come at a much faster rate than what I see now. This is not something we just sit back and think about. Action has to be immediate and very supportive in every sense of the word.

Based on my years of experience the extremes are greater in public schools than they are in private or parochial systems. Whatever the situation and what type of system students attend, we must be educating for the future. The methods of the past were fine for many years. But, the world has moved on and schools must do likewise. The old saying about if it was good enough for me it should be just fine for my children should never be stated in a meaningful way. We know the past has not worked for our students of today and they will certainly not work for what the future is about to bring. Nobody is happy with the old ways of doing things and we should try something new and educationally appropriate. Our investments into the future will foster greater rewards, more challenging courses at the students level and in something the students care more about and have an interest in.

I know it sounds good but it's not just something we should be talking about we have to walk-the-walk and put our money where our mouth is. I have always believed in students being our future. The future is now. Every moment that passes becomes our history and past, the future is the next breath we take. It will never come around again because it will be our past. What the hell are we waiting for? Something else must change with the times is the teaching methods used by our teachers in the classrooms. We have tried to jam math, history, science etc. down the throats of our students for hundreds of years. This is fine for the college prep students but we cannot forget about the vast majority. Will these students ever need the upper level courses in any of these disciplines again? I was on a college prep curriculum in high school and took these upper level courses because I was told to if I ever wanted to be someone. This was all a bunch of you know what and I knew I would never need them again or what I was interested in later in my life. So, why waist my time taking courses I will never use again. I know I can manage the thinking process without taking courses I have no interest in studying in the first place.

After taking the basics and learning to communicate in written and oral form a better way to teach would be getting the non-college prep students in some sort of work-study so they have a skill of some sort when they graduate from high school. With around 90% of our high school graduates never finishing college this type of education would be a lot better suited for them than forcing them into something they have no interest in at all. Teachers would still be needed to teach the basics but after these are learned they can form work-study groups and check and evaluate their student's performances on the job. These work-studies would all receive credit towards graduation and a job once they graduate. What does the average graduate have now? What skills do they possess and who is going to hire them at a rate they can support themselves let alone a family in years to follow? When I was young I had a choice in life. Today there is no choice for students. I could have gone to work in a factory without any skills whatsoever and support a family on my wages and benefits factories were paying. Now, the non-skilled jobs are just not there. Benefits for non-skilled labor are minimal at best. Something must change if children are going to have a future. Things in this country are not getting better. Under the current educational system things never will. We can no longer sit around and wait for the American dream to hit us along side the head. It just doesn't happen in the real world. The American worker of the past is just not needed for the future. Skills will have to be highly developed for the jobs of tomorrow and the place to start is in our schools (K-12).

I believe I was extremely lucky working in the three schools I was employed. The students were their greatest assets. I found out very early in life if students are treated with love and respect along with a caring teacher and administrator they could trust, students will give their best. The real battle ahead is not the students but our conservative outlook by the older generation like their parents and grandparents. Adults are still afraid of anything new while students are willing to take a chance. How many students are far more capable than their parents on a computer today? I had a good secretary who told me if we ever moved away from the typewriter to computers she would not make the change. A year later she decided to retire. This was at Standish-Sterling Central High School and it moved into the 21st. century under my supervision. I have always felt good about that. But for staff members like Mrs. Joan Harmond I must have moved a little to fast for her to handle and understand. She was the type who believed in the old ways of doing things and was totally against change of any type. She had done the same thing with her classes for well over thirty years. This is what put us at opposite extremes from the very beginning of my career at Standish-Sterling. Her mind was made up and she would not listen to any change. I believe if she had her way her students would still be typing on the typewriter and would have never seen a computer. She believed if it was good for her it had to be good for everyone coming her way. I also found out she paid Dave (another Board member) $20,000.00 to go along with her goal of getting rid of me as high school principal. She and Dave would call it a simple loan and never admit it was a payoff for his vote against me. If you remember she stated in Pamida's Department Store she was going to get rid of me no matter what the cost. If it was not a bribe than why would she loan Dave this amount of money knowing his history. I guess I was at least worth that amount and she has never been paid a cent back and she never will. Dave has lived like this since arriving in Standish-Sterling and has not ever paid anyone back for helping him out financially and/or in any other way. I believe this money was a bribe for Dave's vote on the Board. It's actually a small amount to pay for the damage she did in ruining my job and career. As I have stated before she was and is jealous of anyone who lived a better life than she had. I still wonder who she sees in the mirror? I believe it's her mother who was reincarnated in her.

If I had to do it all over again I would have never started my career in education and administration in a parochial system. The salary and benefits along with my retirement was so small I would be living in poverty for the rest of my life. I knew what my calling in life was so I made that choice. The difference in all the three areas above is like night and day. But, the students I met and had a chance to know in a way made it all worthwhile. For as long as I live these memories will stay with me. I did find out no matter where I was at the time students have always been my calling. I do not believe I ever met a student I did not like. I believe there is good in everyone just like there is some bad in others. I did find the students at Standish-Sterling were the ones I respected and liked the most. They were down to earth even though most of them knew they had very little as a group compared to the other two schools. But, even these students didn't seem to know how good they had it. They did not have the money behind most of them but that never mattered. Most of them still knew what life was all about and did what they had to do to survive. They were not out to change the world but just to make their life a little better and there is nothing wrong with that.

I had a good beginning at Bay City All Saints but it did not last long. Father Bob's influence was just too much for me to take. He was with me for a couple of years at St. Stephens in Saginaw and did more damage than he could ever imagine. He tried to be the most popular priest and friend the students could ask for but he actually had the opposite effect. He should try being a priest and not get involved with the younger generation like he did. He just didn't have what it takes when it comes to young students and what they need. Students have their own friends who are usually around their same age. They need someone who cares about them and will be willing to go the extra mile when the time comes. Would I do it all over again? Most likely not! Maybe I should have taken over my father's plumbing and heating business. I would have been my own boss and controlled my own destiny instead of having others do it for me without knowing what they were doing to begin with. I am not a bitter individual who wants to get paid back for anything I have done in my meager life. Now, I just want to be left alone with my family and someday be with my mother once again. Someday this will all take place and I will be satisfied and content with what I have lived and learned in my short time on this planet. As for the individuals I have depicted in this book, I wish them my best because I know they are going to need all the help they can get.

Who knows? Someday I might be taking my story to the public in the form of lectures to college students thinking about becoming an administrator in their future. I believe I can still be a positive influence in the lives of students. They will only hear the truth and never be lied to by me as long as I live.

CONCLUSION

Echoes are everlasting and people must listen to whatever they say. There are many things in one's life and/or the world that just happened for no particular reason. But, in order to live your life you must accept whatever comes and move on. Some believe that there is a plan while others argue that man has a free will and can influence how that plan works out. Life is short and for the most part death will come while we still have something to accomplish.

Our mission in life is like trying to connect two dots in a line. This will usually be done in the shortest line possible. This is why I believe a person must stand for something or die for nothing. What are the important things in life? Can you live and die for honor and self-respect alone? One must establish principles to live by. Without principles in one's life you will lose no matter what. I believe that you should never compromise your principles for money and/or materials things you think you need to live the so-called better life. If mankind is going to survive whatever comes in the future principles must be re-established or we will all lose. If you compromise your principals let's say for a job and more money you lose. In the end, principles establish a code that we live by. This code is also the same things we die by and for.

I have done my best in trying to live my life in as straight a line as possible. I know my time on Earth is as short as it's going to be and for this reason alone I have tried to present only the truth in telling my story. In so doing, I have learned more than I ever wanted to know.

I now realize that friendship is one of the cheapest words in the dictionary. I'm the type of parson who listens a lot to what others are saying. Most of what people talk about are the things they actually know very little about to start with. Friendships are usually just that. They are limited for the most part to and by one's financial status in our society rather than the principles of mankind. Is it because we as a society don't establish a code of conduct and judge people and nations by what they possess? If so, we all lose. True friendship has no limits and no rewards. You just do for your friends because you want to. At times I have stated that I really do not have a friend on this planet.

Most people are not honest and trusting of each other to ever truly establish a true friendship. In saying you care about someone or something there should be no limitation. How many of you can actually say and mean this when you are talking friendship, honesty, caring and trust. Has greed and corruption become the American way of life for most?

I believe living with yourself is our only battle that's worth fighting for. Man doesn't make history but history makes the man. Whatever people do for a living in their lifetime they should never blame anyone else for what happens to them and their career. It has taken me many years to realize that fact. People are as different as night and day. Everyone lives by a different set of principles and codes that determine what's important to and for them.

I see to many people becoming what they hated as a child. They hate their job, family, country and everything in their life. These same things are actually the only things worth fighting for. By changing their life new principles must be established that give you a totally different attitude towards anything coming your way. Sometimes it will take a lifetime to work out if you just sit around and let things happen and do nothing to change your life and make things that will just happen for no particular reason a positive influence on yourself.

The things and individuals that I have written the truth about would have taken place if the individual was I or someone else. Most people can only be responsible for themselves. Their frame of reference has a lot to say as to what people do and how they can live without any feelings whatsoever. I for one have tried to live my life with the principles (pals) I believe in. I have let myself down a few times but I have always tried to bounce back and learn from my mistakes. Living is a learning process that's not inherited. The only important things in my life are the principles of self-respect, honesty, truth and caring for others and things like that.

Echoes were my warning signs that something good and/or bad was about to happen in my life. They were my gut feelings that actually warned me beforehand. I came into this world with absolutely nothing and it looks like I will exit with about the same. I was placed here on Earth to make a difference in young children's lives. I think I have done what has been asked of me. I will continue to be myself and serve the children of God until my dying day. I have actually never wanted to grow up and become someone society has molded. I know the difference between right and wrong along with whom I am. I see way to many people living their life for tomorrow and what might come. What if there was no tomorrow? Live for today for who knows it could be your last.

THOUGHTS TO KEEP IN MIND

Annual evaluations mean absolutely nothing.

Written contracts are not worth the paper they are written on.

Our justice system needs revamping.

Aside from some of your family members, only trust your best friend (Dog or Cat).

Never trust an attorney even if he or she is yours.

Judges use or disregard the laws.

Most people don't care unless they are directly involved.

Loyalty is a two way street and not one-sided.

Most people never tell the truth about anything.

When people lie in court they disrespect the judge and the court.

Honesty and self-respect are all you can bring to the table.

Never put anyone on a pedicle because someday they will fall out of grace.

Most religious leaders preach the Lord's word but have another life.

Local school boards should be eliminated.

Our educational system must change to meet the needs of our country and students.

What was good for you doesn't mean it's good for your children.

Teacher tenure laws only protect the weak and must change.

Unions were good for America way back when but are no longer viable.

Trust comes from within and it's a learned behavior.

Life presents many pathways to follow-you must choose your own.

Looking in a mirror will actually reflect who you are.

People should remain children forever and never grow-up.

Life is like a candle in the wind-it flickers and finally goes out.

Always trust in the Supreme Being first and foremost.

Justice is actually blind in this country and means what it says.

Local, state and national authorities need to do their job. It doesn't work the way you see on television.

It's whom you are that counts and not what others want you to be.

Our American Dream in this country is not for Americans.

History makes the man (woman). Just like the egg came first.

We are born to serve.

We should never judge others without first looking at ourselves.

There are only two days that count in a person's life. The day you are born and Judgment Day.

People should live like there is no tomorrow.

True friends are few and far between.

Know thyself.

My heroes have always been the children.

Gut feelings should never be ignored (Echo).

ABOUT THE AUTHOR

Dennis James Haut is married to his teen sweetheart for the last forty-four years. He would not change one minute of those days with his wife, Gloria for anything. She has always been the one person who brightens up his days. Gloria and Dennis have two children they are extremely proud of. Gary is the oldest while Terri Ann (Haut) Moore is their baby. Gary has not married while Terri has a daughter (Madison) and a son (Nicholas). As a family they are close while being thankful for their children and grandchildren. They both feel they have been blessed.

Dennis has a Bachelor's Degree in Secondary Education and a Master's Degree in Secondary Administration from Central Michigan University. His one hobby is raising, training and judging field trial beagles all over the country.

Dennis spent thirty-four years in the field of education. He became a school administrator early in his career while in the parochial system and finished working in the public school system after spending thirty-two years as a principal from pre-school through grade twelve in two different systems.

Dennis is now retired and working on two additional books entitled "Working The System" and "Repeaters". He guarantees that each book will raise the eyebrows of more than just a few.

CPSIA information can be obtained at www.ICGtesting.com
Printed in the USA
BVOW010431121011

273437BV00001B/43/P